ENOUGH RELIGION TO MAKE US HATE

In Ireland,
enough religion to make us hate,
not enough to make us love.
Jonathan Swift, 1728

Victor Griffin

Enough Religion
to make us hate

REFLECTIONS ON RELIGION AND POLITICS

the columba press

First published in 2002 by
the columba press
55A Spruce Avenue, Stillorgan Industrial Park,
Blackrock, Co Dublin

Cover by Bill Bolger
Origination by The Columba Press
Printed in Ireland by ColourBooks Ltd, Dublin

ISBN 1 85607 360 2

Contents

Prologue

The eccentric Lord Bristol, Frederick Hervey, who was Protestant Bishop of Derry in the eighteenth century and after whom the Hotels Bristol throughout Europe are named to mark his extensive continental tours, built for himself an episcopal palace at Downhill, near Magilligan on the Derry coast overlooking Lough Foyle where it enters the stormy waters of the North Atlantic. The palace is today a ruin, but a temple built on the cliff edge by the bishop in memory of his beloved cousin, Mrs Mussenden, still survives with lines from Lucretius, which appealed to the bishop, carved in the architrave: 'Suave mari magno turbantibus aequora vertis, alterius magnum spectare laborem ...' 'It is sweet when on the great sea the winds are convulsing the waters, to watch another's struggle from the dry land. Not because it delights one that another should be in travail, but because it is a relief to observe what trials you have not to endure!' And so say all of us (the retired).

From the Downhill cliffs, Inishowen in Donegal seems only a stone's throw away across Lough Foyle, that narrow water marking the dividing line between Northern Ireland and the Irish Republic. I am fortunate in that I feel equally at home in both jurisdictions. Twenty two years in Derry, followed by another twenty two in St Patrick's Cathedral, Dublin, have given me a sense of belonging, of never feeling a stranger in a strange land. I can feel equally at home and at ease when I join in 'The Soldiers' Song' in Croke Park or in 'God save the Queen' on Remembrance Sunday in Limavady. Some may find this impossible, self contradictory, schizophrenic. I can only say this is how it is for me, equally at home and at ease with both traditions.

7

Which seems to show that identity is not a simple straightforward issue. I believe we have defined it too narrowly, too negatively – who and what we *are not* or *against* rather than who and what we *are for*. Irishness as anti-British; Northern Ireland unionism not only as anti-nationalism and republicanism, but even anti-Irish. Southern Irish unionists including Carson had no hesitation in being Irish *and* British. There was no inherent contradiction. For the sake of simplicity or prejudice, we conveniently close our eyes to how much we owe to each other, how much the two nationalities, British (especially the English) and the Irish are intertwined. And of course, Scotland and Northern Ireland have always had a particularly close relationship even before the time of St Columba. Therefore the whole concept of identity, especially in this age of the global village and the European Union, needs to be seen in terms of positive enrichment rather than negative exclusion.

Born in a small town, Carnew, near the Wicklow/Wexford border, I was given the name Victor after Queen Victoria who had the same birthday and also after Victoria Street, Dublin, where we had close relatives. My father, a man of many parts, farmer, shopkeeper, motor engineer, funeral undertaker, who brought the first wireless set and electric light to Carnew, was a risk taker, incurably reckless, never interested in making money, widely known for his generosity to all and sundry. Although a devout member of the Church of Ireland, religious denomination was always secondary to him for all were children of the one God, equally loved and valued by the one God and Father of us all. When the Angelus rang he would say to his Roman Catholic helpers, 'Now you say *your* prayers and I'll say *mine*.'

My mother came from a family of small farmers in Co Monaghan. She had a flair for fashion and after some time as a milliner in Clones, moved south to Carnew to become a millinery buyer in a departmental store. She was practical, frugal, a necessary foil to an audacious and unpredictable husband, in complete and competent control of the domestic and financial front. I have a sheaf of unpaid bills in her neat handwriting – it was she who kept the accounts – held together by a large, long-since-rusted safety pin, itemising the account to the Carnew IRA in October 1922 for the hire of cars, many of them having come back to the garage the worse for wear during the civil war.

While segregation, 'them and us', was the rule in schools and churches, thankfully it never obtained in the local farming and business community. Protestants and Roman Catholics mingled together, would drop into each others' homes for an evening fireside chat, when the talk usually centred on the price of bullocks, the state of the crops, recent marriages and deaths. The only hint of embarrassment came when there was a mixed marriage. Both sides remained silent. I suppose by a sort of tacit mutual agreement mention of such matters was ruled out. The unjust *Ne Temere* decree meant that all the children had to be brought up as Roman Catholics, causing a marked decline in the Protestant population and much resentment at the Roman Catholic Church. Even at this early boyhood stage I felt it uncomfortably strange to think that the Christian religion, which should have been a loving and unifying force, was the great issue dividing Protestant from Catholic, Christian from Christian. How untrue to the teaching of its founder. I used to wonder, what has gone wrong? How can this be in so-called Christian Ireland, the island of saints and scholars?

As time went on I began to see that the institutional churches, with their politicised religion, self righteous triumphalism and exclusive superiority, had a lot to answer for. Years later Swift came to mind: 'In Ireland we have enough religion to make us hate but not enough to make us love.'

In the overwhelming Roman Catholic ethos of the new independent Ireland Protestants, a beleaguered minority, felt vulnerable, not really accepted as the 'genuine article', associated in the public mind with the British ascendancy. Understandably they kept a low profile, their heads down, especially when it came to religion and politics. And there were other distinguishing features.

The only unsupervised freedom I experienced during my

time at Kilkenny College was as a chorister in St Canice's when we were allowed to walk to the cathedral and return on our own. Arrayed on Sundays in Eton suits and mortar boards, Kilkenny boys were figures of fun or, at the very least, objects of curiosity to the local populace. 'Proddy Woddy cups and saucers', jeered some in reference to our religion and our mortar boards. This unusual garb served to increase our sense of alien- ation. Not only did we attend a Protestant school, but we were compelled to wear the badge of our peculiar separateness.

Courtown Harbour was our mecca during the summer holi- days. On Sundays and church feast days, such as 29 June and 15 August, swimmers and splashers, farmers and their families made this pilgrimage, many on the off-chance of meeting some friends, distant cousins or old acquaintances. Weather-beaten sons of the soil, Protestant and Catholic, dressed in Sunday best, would sit together on the wall gazing out to sea, discussing the price of land or bullocks or the state of the crops. Then at the ap- proach of darkness all were homeward bound, except the cinema goers and dance-hallers. But for Protestants, no cinema or dance-hall. Such breaking of the Sabbath was frowned on in Protestant circles, and any infringement was seen as a lukewarm attitude to the faith and the first step on the road to a mixed mar- riage with the inevitable and dreaded consequence of capitul- ation to Rome.

Protestant thoughts were occasionally turned from the dom- estic religious scene when a returned missionary would arrive, complete with magic lantern and bulky slides of foreign parts. Huddled together in a darkened classroom, with the hissing and pungent smell of carbide as the lantern was activated, we gazed in awe and admiration on one who had actually been to Africa or Asia and escaped the cannibals' cauldron. The last slide was always the words of a missionary hymn. As the piano thumped out the tune we all joined in. Our pennies and sixpences clinked on the collecting plate and the strains of 'From Greenland's Icy Mountains' reverberated over the silent street outside. We were left in no doubt that the poor, blind, 'benighted heathen, bowing down to wood and stone' needed us to lighten their darkness. We must be prepared to bear the 'white man's burden' and from our lofty spiritual pinnacle look down and be ready to introduce the 'lesser breeds' to the benefits of Western Christian civilisation, of the WASP (White Anglo Saxon Protestant) variety of course. And 'the one true church' refrain was equally trumpeted by our Roman Catholic neighbours in competition for the salvation of poor black African souls. Here was the heyday of institutional religion, Protestant and Roman Catholic alike, dogmatic, confident, self assured, having the whole truth and each utterly convinced that they had nothing to learn from 'the others'.

Playing or watching games of any sort on Sundays was then out of the question, a flagrant breach of the Sabbath. Rugby, which many Protestants played, was then a Saturday sport. It never occurred to Protestants that the biblical Sabbath fell on Saturday and to be true to the literal interpretation of the commandment Saturday sport should have been ruled out. No biblical restriction could be applied to Sunday sport.

At Kilkenny the uncharacteristically liberal decision to allow boys to play tennis on Sunday afternoons had caused uproar among some parents who protested, in vain, that their sons were being encouraged to break the Sabbath. In addition to playing their games on Sundays, the nationalist ethos of the GAA did not appeal to Protestants, who associated the organisation with the Roman Catholic Church and a very extreme form of anti-British republicanism. The GAA ban preventing its members playing, or even attending, non-Gaelic games also meant that the few Protestants who might have ignored their community's disapproval of 'Sabbath' sport and taken up hurling or football were unwilling to forego their rugby, hockey, soccer or cricket to comply with GAA regulations. Passing Croke Park on my way from Mountjoy School, then in Mountjoy Square, to our sports field in Clontarf, I was bewildered by an attitude which decreed that to be truly Irish one had to renounce all interest in 'foreign' games.

Little did I know that years later I would probably be the first

Protestant clergyman, certainly the first Dean of St Patrick's, to make my way to a GAA final there, and on a Sunday too.

After austere Kilkenny College and relaxed Mountjoy School, Dublin, came Trinity in 1942, then very much a Protestant, indeed unionist university, since large numbers of students from the Protestant and unionist tradition came from Northern Ireland. Presbyterian Divinity students from Magee College, Derry, took Trinity degrees, having spent the two years leading up to the final exam in Trinity. The Church of Ireland Divinity School was included in the university faculties. The unionist students on the college roof gave full vent to their loyalty to the crown on VE Day, which resulted in the burning of the union flag by republicans in College Green, followed by the burning of the Irish tricolour by the students, my first direct experience of unionist/republican conflict.

In 1947 and for the next twenty two years ministering in Derry city, this tension became part and parcel of the segregated society of Northern Ireland, at times flaring into open confrontation but always there smouldering beneath the surface. Here was politicised religion masquerading as Christianity, with unionism solidly wedded to Protestantism and nationalism to Roman Catholicism. And Protestant unionism let it be known in an unmistakable manner that it was in the ascendancy. The tacit acceptance of a Catholic state for a Catholic people in the twenty six counties was matched by a 'Protestant parliament for a Protestant people' in the six. Fear and the siege mentality of unionism inevitably led to discrimination, the 'them and us' mentality, potential traitors as against trustworthy loyalists. I voiced opposition to the Stormont unionist government for its neglect of Derry and the north west. The new university went to Coleraine, and the GNR railway via Omagh to Portadown was closed without anything like the financial investment provided to improve the roads in the north west being available compared to what was taking place in the east of the province with its extensive construction of motorways and dual carriageways. This opposition to Stormont, together with the suggestion that power sharing should take place in the Derry corporation, and/or party labels should be abolished so that all citizens could identify with the city and work together for its welfare, led to accusations of Griffin 'the Fenian' or 'Lundy' from the more extreme Protestant unionist adherents.

And, of course, Protestant clergy who tried to promote ecumenism and the gospel message of reconciliation involving co-operation, mutual respect and an end to the evil of sectarianism, were likewise called 'children of the devil'. In Northern Ireland the tail usually wags the dog. The majority, for whatever reason, fear to say publicly what they have no hesitation saying privately. Tunnel visioned minorities with their simplistic solutions, these political activists had an influence, for example in elections, far exceeding their numerical and totally committed adherents. Political and religious tribalism, condoned if not actively supported by the churches, in the end 'called the tune' and Jesus of Nazareth, with his message of love and inclusiveness, was so often left out in the cold. No room for him in the northern inn.

In 1969, having spent twenty two years in the North, on returning to the Republic I found a general atmosphere of complacency and indeed self congratulation on having a society which, if not perfect, needed very little, if any change when compared to Northern Ireland. While the sight of politics dominating religion, especially unionism hand in hand with Protestantism in the North was utterly abhorrent to the citizens of the Republic, the idea of religion dominating politics in the Republic and the Catholic ethos of the state was generally accepted as an essential of true Irishness, if not enthusiastically endorsed.

I began to say things like 'our own backyard also needs some cleaning up' and suggested we should try to understand the unionist point of view, treat it seriously and cultivate an attitude of respect for diversity and inclusiveness. In a word, that we should move towards a more open, tolerant and pluralist society, recognising and embracing different traditions and cultures as an enrichment of the whole body politic, and in which no church should have a dominant role. This was something new. The sparks soon began to fly. 'Griffin is another Paisley,' said a TD in Dáil Éireann who was enraged by my criticism of the role of the Roman Catholic Church in politics in the Republic. I could not help a wry smile when I remembered the accolade 'Griffin the Fenian' bestowed on me by fanatical Protestant unionists in the North. But much support also was forthcoming from across the religious divide.

Following on from the idea of a pluralist society which I advocated during the 1970s, I had no hesitation later on in opposing the insertion into the Constitution of an amendment to prohibit abortion without any exceptions, which to add insult to injury was also highly ambiguous, and I supported the 1986 proposal to remove the constitutional ban on divorce.

The old Liberties quarter of Dublin, around St Patrick's, was being allowed to deteriorate with residents removed to new housing estates on the outskirts of the city. To oppose what we saw as the systematic destruction of the old historic Dublin, a number of us banded together to form the Dublin Crisis Conference.

Until the Wood Quay controversy in 1978 there really was no widespread interest in preserving our architectural or archaeological heritage. Wood Quay was a watershed. Only then did people become alarmed at the destruction of Dublin and decide that it was time to call a halt.

A few brave voices, such as that of Deirdre Kelly, had protested at the destruction of Dublin but the property speculators and road engineers were undeterred. There was also a political dimension. Why preserve the relics, the reminders of the Anglo-Irish Establishment, Georgian or Victorian, in this newly created independent state? Better to demolish and replace by something more in keeping with Irish culture. Anglo-Irish must be replaced by Gaelic. There was no question of co-existing or being mutually enriching. Authentic Irishness was exclusive, not inclusive. Brits out!

In 1985 a number of us who were concerned at the deterioration of the city met together and arranged a conference, the Dublin Crisis Conference, which was held in February 1986 in the old Synod Hall in Christchurch Place. We met in Larry Dillon's house in the Coombe and also present were Frank McDonald, Deirdre and Aidan Kelly, Mick Rafferty, David Norris and Donal Storey.

The conference theme was, 'What's wrong with Dublin – why it's wrong and what can be done about it?' At the conference we had a large and representative attendance. For the first time people from interested environmental groups from all over the city came together and major recommendations emerged. The findings of that conference, and the enthusiasm which was apparent, received wide publicity and support and the result was 'Manifesto for the city', dealing with a host of issues such as public transport, roads, pedestrianisation, renewal of the inner city, facilities for youth, the old, the disabled, etc.

The proposal to construct a dual carriageway outside the West Front of St Patrick's had grave and frightening implications for the cathedral. Apparently the planners had never seriously considered the possibility of damage to the cathedral's foundation and fabric by an increased traffic flow along a 90 feet wide carriageway, or the added risk to the safety of our children in our cathedral schools by the resultant pollution of the immediate environment, including noise pollution. I drew up a submission to the Corporation setting out in detail these and other relevant points and suggested an alternative 'one-way' traffic system for the area which would facilitate a pedestrianisation of that portion of Patrick Street immediately outside the cathedral and Choir School. This was promptly rejected by the planners, who assured me that the experts on such matters were completely satisfied that no harm would result to the cathedral's foundation or fabric by increased traffic flow and vibration. How on earth, I wondered, could any expert predict, be he ever so competent, what might or might not happen to a building which had stood intact for 800 years when suddenly subjected to the incessant pounding of heavy traffic on its perimeter? However, the planners were determined to have their way and the Corporation ready to rubber stamp their recommendations.

I decided we would have to fight this to the bitter end. We held street protest meetings and I took to the soap box and megaphone outside the cathedral, after which on one Monday evening, led by a Liberties bagpiper, a vast concourse of Liberties dwellers and supporters from all over the city (Ulick O'Connor, Siobhan McKenna, and others were present to add voice and encouragement) and members of the Dublin Crisis Committee, converged on the City Hall to lobby the members of the Corporation. More speeches were made. TV cameras were present and our cause received national publicity. Noel Carroll, the Corporation's PRO, referred to us as 'articulate loud-mouths', resisting progress and refusing to face reality.

The planners were unmoved. They knew better than the citizens. They were the experts. The Corporation, with some honourable exceptions such as Carmencita Hederman, believed this and trusted them. At this stage, when all seemed lost, I decided to appeal to Charles Haughey, leader of Fianna Fáil, who had at that time a majority in the Dublin Corporation. I remembered that I had willingly agreed some months before to a suggestion by Mr Haughey that a scene from a TV video production, 'Charles Haughey's Ireland', might feature the historic Deanery as a venue for a conversation between the two of us on the contribution made by Swift and other Protestant patriots to Ireland. The film had a wide circulation and I received some feedback, not all complimentary, for some were critical of my alleged support of Charles Haughey and Fianna Fáil. I might add that I would have been equally willing to appear with any other political leader in conversation in the Deanery had a similar request been made.

On the maxim that 'one good turn deserves another', I picked up the phone and rang Mr Haughey, who listened carefully as I put my case and he promised to try and achieve a mutually acceptable solution. On the following Monday the Corporation, with the support of the Fianna Fáil members, decided to reconsider the question of the dual carriageway. Shortly afterwards I was invited by Mr Haughey to his home in Kinsealy, and when I arrived with Arthur West, our engineer, and Trevor Matthews (now Councillor) representing the Cathedral Board, officials of the various planning departments were present, together with Mr Bertie Ahern. Mr Haughey had prepared meticulously for the meeting. An imposing, large-scale, well-constructed and accurate model of the cathedral and dual carriageway occupied centre floor in the spacious room. We all gathered round and the pros and cons were discussed. All were anxious to reach agreement and put an end to public confrontation. Eventually Mr Haughey produced the compromise by removing from the model the section of the dual carriageway outside the cathedral and Choir School and suggesting a narrower road at a distance of forty-five feet from the existing cathedral railings, with the intervening space to be pedestrianised or treated in a manner in keeping with the cathedral's environs. Other related matters, such as limited traffic access to the Close, were agreed. I attempted to raise the question of reducing the width of the Clanbrassil Street carriageway but this was ruled out by Mr Haughey, who insisted we confine our attention to Patrick Street.

However, due to continuing local pressure, the Clanbrassil carriageway was eventually reduced in width from ninety to sixty feet. I was in the gallery when the amended Patrick Street proposal came before the Corporation. It was a stormy meeting. Feelings ran high. Accusations were flung across the chamber. 'Who does Mr Haughey think he is? Who is running this city, the Corporation or Charlie Haughey and Dean Griffin? Are all future decisions to be made in Kinsealy?' Whatever the procedural rights or wrongs may have been, I shall always be grateful to Mr Haughey for his intervention and his determination to safeguard St Patrick's Cathedral. Were we witnessing the end of the old era when public bodies, corporations and councils, accepted without adequate scrutiny the recommendations of their planning 'experts' and simply applied the rubber stamp? If so, our protest and the efforts of the lone courageous voices crying in the wilderness for many years, such as Deirdre and Aidan

Kelly, were not in vain. In all our protests religious differences were transcended. Denomination was irrelevant, a fine example of practical ecumenism.

Less successful were my efforts to share St Patrick's by persuading other denominations to use the cathedral on a regular basis for services according to their own rites, as a witness to our unity in Christ as one family under the one Fatherhood of God. In other words, to make St Patrick's a truly national, inclusive, ecumenical cathedral. I am confident that one day this will be achieved and that instead of seeking security in the past, we shall venture forth in faith like wise men following a star to Bethlehem.

How often has it been said that we in Ireland suffer the burden or legacy of our history? The trouble is that we interpret present facts in the light of our perception of the past, making past conflicts, isolated from their historical context, suit present prejudices. Thus the myth or half truth takes the place of reality. For the diehard nationalist, republican, unionist or Orangeman the past as he sees it, so often with squinted vision, must dominate the present and fashion the future. To think or do otherwise would betray the memory of the dead – based on the unwarranted assumption that the dead heroes of 1798 or 1916 or 1690 would think and act in exactly the same way if alive today. This is the road to nowhere, except to bigotry and intolerance, whether political or religious, stemming from a smug dogmatic self-righteousness.

The segregation in the education of children on religious grounds, encouraging however unwittingly a 'them and us' attitude, with no exposure in the classroom to the other tradition, has also helped to keep conflicting prejudices and myths alive and well. Lord Londonderry, the first Northern Ireland Minister for Education, saw that integrated or multi-denominational schools were necessary, especially in Northern Ireland, to help defeat the prevailing distrust and division and assist the cause of reconciliation. For him it was essential to begin with bringing the children together, seeing them as one family under one God.

But the churches, both Protestant and Roman Catholic, would have none of it and in exclusive denominational schools, myths, prejudice and half truths found a conducive and unchallenged happy hunting ground, so often aided and abetted by sectarianism in the home, all of which produced in the more impressionable and pliant minds an intense hatred of the other side and the resolve to do something about it by following in the footsteps of their dead heroes, whether loyalist or republican.

Thus in Christian Ireland, the island of saints and scholars, Swift's immortal and terrible words ring in our ears: 'In Ireland, enough religion to make us hate, but not enough (Christianity) to make us love.'

CHAPTER I

Absolutism: The Perversion of Christianity

The aforesaid Frederick Hervey, Earl of Bristol and eccentric Bishop of Derry in the eighteenth century, believed in God but hardly in religion. He was really a deist, believing that God created the universe, but had left the running of it entirely to his creatures without any divine intervention. In the moral ordering of things, so the bishop contended, mankind can find assistance not only in the Bible, particularly in the life, example and teaching of Jesus, but also in the ancient Greek and Latin authors, Plato, Aristotle, Lucretius, Cicero etc. Thus for the earl bishop there was no divine sanction for any particular religion or denomination. No one true church. Religion in most cases was decided merely by an accident of birth. In his case the Church of England which he formally adhered to, taking full advantage of its comprehensiveness, was for him as good as any. It suited his nature. After the accident of birth, it really all comes down to a matter of taste. What suits one, won't suit another, so the bishop believed. Those with a craving for absolute certainty will be more at home, say, in ultramontanism or 'infallible conservative' Roman Catholicism or biblical fundamentalist Protestantism than, for example, in untidy Anglicanism.

Therefore, the earl bishop concluded there must be tolerance if we are to have a peaceful and ordered society. Accordingly, he disapproved of discrimination against Roman Catholics, gave financial help to the building of Roman Catholic churches, made available on his estate a venue for the saying of Mass, and took responsibility for payment of a priest.

Jonathan Swift was well aware of the hatred generated by religion. But he concurred with the accepted idea that, for peace and security in society, each state must have an official or established church to which all citizens were required to conform under penalty of persecution or even death. It may be Anglicanism as in England and Ireland, or Roman Catholicism in France or Spain, or Calvinism in Geneva. However, Swift's biting satirical treatment of the establishment, whether political or religious, had the long term effect of diminishing respect for official and established state religion, thereby inevitably leading to tolerance for all religions with freedom for those of any religion, or none, to act according to their conscience within the law.

Tolerance is not a negative attitude, grudgingly conceding the right of others to hold beliefs which differ from ours (toleration might be an appropriate term for this), but a positive attitude welcoming the diversity of views as mutually enriching and stimulating. Without tolerance there can be no respect for others. Without respect there can be no mutual understanding. Without mutual understanding there can be no reconciliation. Without reconciliation there can be no love, either of God or my neighbour. The child of intolerance is hatred – enough religion to make us hate.

When all is said and done there are only two absolutes, love of God and love of my neighbour. Religious sectarianism rears its ugly head when we absolutise our particular interpretation of the meaning and application of the gospel as the only one true valid one, and worship the dogmas and doctrines which we have formulated, instead of worshipping the one God and Father of us all. In the end we have only our particular viewpoint or perspective. All we are justified in saying is, 'This is how it appears to me. You may have a different point of view and I must respect it.' It is highly unlikely that the wise men on returning home from Bethlehem would have described the same baby Jesus in exactly the same way to their friends. One would have noted or emphasised a particular feature and his companion another. We are all sinners and flawed in our religion and politics. All we can say is 'God be merciful to me, a sinner.' Never 'Thank God I'm not like the other crowd.' The worship-

ping of slogans, religious or political and their use by fanatical
so-called Christians to attack the other side, is the modern idolatry.

So often we try to fashion God as we would like him to be,
make him to suit ourselves, in our image. We make him synonymous with the institution. But God is not in our hands. We are in
God's hands and he will not be bound by any chains or strict-
ures which we place on his love and justice. We try to hold him
in the doctrinal and church institutional tombs which we have
constructed but God will not be bound by human dogma. He
will always break loose in resurrection glory. This is the sure
ground of our faith and hope and charity. The great danger of
the institutional churches is the temptation to 'hi-jack' Jesus,
tame him, control him, make him do our bidding instead of us
doing his, make the church the Lord of Christ instead of Christ
the Lord of the church.

Bearing this in mind, isn't it about time that we in all our
churches, in the spirit of repentance and reconciliation, removed
from our confessional statements that which is negative and offensive to fellow Christians, e.g. referring to the Pope as the anti-
Christ (Presbyterian Westminster Confession) or to 'sacrifices of
masses as blasphemous fables and dangerous deceits' (Anglican
39 Articles) or to Anglican Holy Orders as 'absolutely null and
utterly void' (Roman Catholic *Apostolicae Curae* by Leo XIII, 1896).
Such doctrinal sniping at one another can hardly be calculated
to increase the effectiveness of the churches' witness in a secular
and sceptical age. Religion serves as a vehicle for hatred when
offensive confessional statements, taken literally and out of their
historical context, are eagerly seized on by fanatics to fuel the
fires of sectarian hatred. And in these days of the global village
in a pluralist world with so many varieties – ethnic, religious,
cultural, political – all having to share the same planet, it is essential that our ecumenism be extended to reach out to others of different faiths and cultures. For all the major religions emphasise
love, compassion, mercy and tolerance with which Christians
can identify. The precepts of the Bible, the Koran, or the holy

books of India or China, have so much in common that we can echo the words of William Blake :

'All must love the human form
In Heathen, Turk or Jew
Where mercy, love and pity dwell
There God is dwelling too.'

Pope John Paul, on the theme of inter-religious dialogue (October 2000), said: 'God who is the Father of all, offers the gift of salvation to all the nations. Under the influence of the Holy Spirit, who is also at work outside the limits of the church, people in every part of the world seek to adore God in an authentic way. The religious texts of other religions point to a future of communion with God, of purification and salvation; and they encourage people to seek the truth and defend the values of life, holiness, justice, peace and freedom. When Christians engage in inter-religious dialogue, they bring with them their faith in Jesus Christ, the only Saviour of the world. This same faith teaches them to recognise the authentic religious experience of others and to listen to them in the spirit of humility, in order to discover and appreciate every ray of truth, from wherever it comes.'

No longer must we aim to convert 'the heathen in his blindness' as when we viewed the world as divided between Christian/civilised and pagan/uncivilised, and even worse between true Christianity (ours) and erroneous Christianity (theirs). Instead we must concentrate on giving to and receiving insight and inspiration from each other to our mutual enrichment. God is father of all and all are equally loved by him. The *Logos*, the Word, is not limited but, as St John says, 'lightens every person coming into the world'.

Christians are only entitled to say that the religion in which they have been brought up or have embraced is the true way as they see it, true for them, and to recognise that the Moslems, Hindus, Buddhists and others are also entitled to say the same about the religion or the atheism in which they have been nourished or have embraced. All are of course entitled to try and persuade others by word and example to see 'the truth' as they perceive it. As finite human beings, absolute truth is really beyond our comprehension. We can 'know only in part', as St Paul puts it. Humility, not arrogance, is required. What we can say is that as civilised mature persons we approach nearest to the Absolute, God's nature, God's truth revealed as love, when we resolve to treat each individual of whatever creed, colour or class as the child of God, each of infinite value in God's sight, and aim to give expression to this in all our political and social structures.

Absolutism or fundamentalism is really a reduction of the majesty of the deity to fit the narrow dogmatism of human minds, with their frightening conviction that to them belongs the one true interpretation of the divine will, with all others seen as erroneous or indeed satanic. Such absolutism, which has caused so much misery, hatred and bloodshed, brings all religion into disrepute – a God of love no longer universal and global but tribal and sectarian. The realisation that God is greater than all our theological dogmas will inevitably result in a measure of true humility, real tolerance, fruitful co-operation and co-existence, to our mutual understanding and enrichment. For God is always fugitive and will always escape from our dogmatic nets.

We are all born with a certain colour, into a particular creed, class or culture. While we should recognise, indeed celebrate, what is best in such diversity as an enrichment to society, we should beware of falling into the attitude of claiming that our colour, creed or class is superior to others. There must be respect for the dignity and sanctity of the human person as such, whoever, whatever, wherever he or she may be. In Christianity and other world faiths, this dignity is grounded in the belief that each person has the stamp of the divine image, a child of the one heavenly Father and one whom God loves as if he had no-one else to love. Once absolutist claims to political, racial or religious supremacy take over, the inherent worth of each human person is denied. Ideology and dogmatism demand that 'the others' are inferior and as such have either to conform, be enslaved or, in the final analysis, be exterminated as in the Nazi concentration camps. They have no right to continue to exist as they are. Indeed the mark of civilisation is really the ability and willingness to empathise, to feel with and for others who are perhaps of a different race, religion or culture. The Nazi SS who murdered millions of Jews had lost this ability to feel, to identity, to internalise the pain they were causing to others. Here we see evil and a loss of humanity. There is no humanity where there is deliberate cruelty and a loss of identity in particular with fellow human beings, the inability to feel the suffering of others.

The history of religion tragically is stained by the persecution and execution of so-called heretics or dissidents, carried out at the command of those who fervently believed not only that they were in possession of the one true faith, but that they also had a divine sanction to impose their convictions on others by deprivation of human rights, torture and finally, if all else failed, death by sword, hanging or burning. This also served as a warning to others. Cromwell, so convinced of the rightness of his puritan convictions, would tolerate no dissent and firmly believed that he was doing the will of God by silencing or annihilating his opponents. At the other end of the spectrum, Sir Thomas More, now canonised as a saint and recently made the Patron Saint of politicians, while devout and splendidly courageous even to death in defence of his faith and conscience, was totally opposed to extending such freedom of conscience to others. Consequently he had no hesitation in systematically, without mercy, torturing 'the heretics'. Heresy for him (as indeed for Cromwell) was an offence against 'the one true church' and, as a grievous sin against God and the truth, it must be rooted out.

And so the Christianity of Jesus of Nazareth, with his emphasis on the infinite worth of each person in God's sight, and his gospel of mutual respect, tolerance for diversity, compassion and inclusiveness, became perverted into one of intolerance and exclusiveness, with an arrogant and self righteous hatred of any who for whatever reason felt unable to conform to the established order in church or state.

The true follower of Christ really belongs totally to no one particular denomination. He belongs to all and all belong to him for in Christ he transcends that of which he is a member. Therefore he is open minded, willing to listen, learn and understand; careful never to hurt; rejoicing in communion with fellow Christians; conscious of our doctrinal imperfections for as the apostle Paul says, 'Here we know only in part and our pronouncements are in part' (1 Corinthians 13:9). Accordingly no denomination can ever be the sole possessor of the whole truth, or claim supremacy over all the rest.

Under the guidance of the Holy Spirit, the churches have been led to view Christians in other traditions in a manner different from our ancestors. For example, in the sixteenth century it was regarded as the right and religious thing to burn heretics. Slavery, and the supposed inferiority of black people, was not felt to be contrary to the gospel for many centuries. So the Holy Spirit leads us into a deeper understanding of the mind of Christ and enables us in time to correct what is missing and supply what is lacking in our Christian witness.

All confessional statements, such as on the nature of the church or Christian ministry, must therefore be seen in their historical context and not as absolutes, valid for all time. To treat them as timeless absolutes is really to deny the ongoing work of the Holy Spirit, ever leading us to a deeper insight into the meaning, implication and contemporary relevance of the one truth revealed to us in Jesus Christ.

St Paul, in his second letter to the Corinthians, says that we have the treasure of the gospel 'in earthen or common clay vessels'(2 Corinthians 4:7). The vessel, the institutional church, is only the means, the vessel of clay, fragile, in constant need of repair and renovation. We must never regard it as the end, nor equate it with the treasure who is Jesus, the same, yesterday and for ever. If Jesus were to come back today one can only imagine how perplexed, even incensed, he would be at all the dogmas, definitions, attempts at theological justification taking precedence over and indeed often conflicting with his simple message of love for God and love, care and compassion for all God's creatures.

Jesus emphasised the provisional status of all systems, religious and moral. 'The Sabbath (the system) was made for man, not man for the Sabbath,' he declared. He suffered at the hands of those who sought to impose authoritarianism and legalism in the name of God. They were determined to maintain their institutional power and prestige, and those who questioned their authoritarianism suffered their wrath and condemnation.

Jesus certainly did not set up a system or found a community which can be identified with the institutional complexity of the church as it later became, a religious organisation based on controlling and excluding people from God by legalism. This was in stark contrast to the inclusiveness favoured by Jesus, based on compassion for each individual and the breaking down of every barrier of division or separateness.

The absolutising of the institution or the means whereby the gospel is communicated is what the Bible calls idolatry, making the relative absolute. Either the church itself with its dogmas, rituals and ceremonies, or the very text of Holy Scripture regarded as the inerrant and infallible Word of God, become idols.

In the former, Jesus, the Word of God, is identified with the institutional church, while in the latter, Jesus, the Word of God, is identified with the text of Holy Scripture.

CHAPTER 2

Christ and Caesar, Hand in Glove

The church, said Lord Acton, 'began with the principle of liberty both as her claim and as her rule'.

Alas, in time this principle was soon eroded when worldly power and institutional pride replaced humility and lost sight of what St Paul describes as 'the glorious liberty of the children of God'. (Romans 8:21)

St Paul warned the Corinthians that there was to be no forcing of consciences since the freedom brought by Christ applied to all. In the church there would be no more Jew or Gentile, slave or free, male or female, but all one in Jesus Christ. The Christian must respect others in a spirit of love based on freedom, for all were free as the children of God.

Externally Christians were to be free from political repression and persecution, since according to Christ they were to fulfil all their obligations to the state, rendering 'to Caesar that which is Caesar's and to God that which is God's'. Secular government and religion were to be separate, and the state had no right to interfere with religion, as long as its laws were obeyed and its obligations met. Absolute distinction of church and state became the charter of Christian claims to toleration under the Roman Empire. When Christians, like members of other religions, carried out their secular duties, the state had no right to interfere with the consciences of individual Christians who in times of persecution were prepared to meet death rather than deny their Christian faith.

For two centuries the fathers of the Christian and Catholic Church continued to demand toleration on this basis. 'By both human and natural law,' Tertullian protested in the third century, 'each one is free to adore whom he wants. The religion of an individual neither harms nor profits anybody else. It is against the nature of religion to force religion.'

In 313 AD the Roman Empire under Constantine finally gave official toleration to Christians and in due course the established religion, Christianity, was drawn irresistibly towards an alliance of interest with the secular power. The new church-state alliance then began a programme of selective persecution. The Roman emperors outlawed paganism and pulled down its altars. By the end of the fourth century the church was supporting persecution against heterodox Christians or 'heretics'. The church looked with approval on the measures taken by the secular authorities against the Arians and the Donatists. 'There is an unjust persecution which the ungodly operate against the church of Christ; and a just persecution which the churches of Christ make use of towards the ungodly. The church persecutes out of love, the ungodly out of cruelty'. Thus said Augustine, Bishop of Hippo, who was to prove a powerful authority for later protagonists of religious intolerance. 'Compel them to come in' (Luke 14:23) was for him a definitive scriptural text justifying the persecution of heretics.

The basis of intolerance in the Middle Ages was the alliance between church and state. With the demise of the old Empire the church had become the unique upholder of civilisation in Europe. In his Bull, *Unam Sanctam*, in 1302 Boniface VIII claimed that all authority on earth was vested in the church; two swords ruled the world, but both swords, the spiritual and the material, were in the power of the church.

Fortified by this sovereignty in temporal matters, the church did not hesitate to persecute heresies that allegedly threatened the temporal order. Church and state made common cause against heterodox preaching to preserve the doctrinal and social unity of Christendom. Pope and Emperor had a mutual interest in having a strong central authority both in state and church enforcing a rigid uniformity and quickly disposing of any signs of dissidence. Thus the pattern of the Roman empire with its strong central authority in Rome in the person of the Emperor, enforcing uniformity throughout its domains, became the pattern of the Roman Church with its strong central authority in Rome, in the person of the Pope, enforcing uniformity throughout the various churches.

This pattern continued right into the Reformation period. Conformity in faith implied unity and security in society. To differ in faith meant to threaten the fabric of society. Both church and state consequently set their face against dissidents, religious or political. However, non-Christians were theoretically free from persecution. Christians could and did co-exist peaceably with Jews and Muslims in several parts of the Mediterranean world, in spite of the Spanish Inquisition and periods of intense persecution, especially during Holy Week with the plundering of ghettos, burning of synagogues, sadly often condoned or approved by the church on the grounds that the Jews were the murderers of Christ, indeed of God, and had at the crucifixion loudly boasted 'His blood be on us and on our children'. (Matthew 27:25) 'This will follow the Jewish people as a curse where they live and work, when they are born and when they die,' said Pope Innocent III (1215). The rights of conscience were not explicitly recognised by medieval theologians. The objective law of God, as laid down by the church, was the sole criterion of right action, and a conscience which went against that law sinned. The Christian humanist Erasmus (1509), however, was unhappy about persecution. He advocated fewer dogmas: 'The sum of our religion is peace, but this can only come about when we define as little as possible and leave the judgment free on many matters; besides there is the immense obscurity of very many questions.' He was the opponent of rigidity, inflexibility and religious legalism. The reactionary Catholics looked on him with suspicion, as did Luther.

Luther, Calvin and Zwingli, the three principal names in the official Reformation, were lukewarm on the concept of religious liberty for it could get out of hand and endanger the social order. Despite these reformers' lack of support, the Reformation did bring in time greater religious liberty. Lecky the historian points out that 'toleration, however incompatible with some of the tenets which Protestants have asserted, is essentially a normal result of Protestantism, for it is the direct, logical and inevitable consequence of the due exercise of private judgment'. Luther and Calvin closely identified church and state and accordingly rejected the idea of religious and social diversity. But the individualism of other reformers, for example the Anabaptists, who had looked to the Reformation for greater liberty and tolerance, expressed itself in open discontent and even rebellion. The conservative reformers, far from breaking clear of the notion of an established church to which all must conform, had reasserted it with vigour.

In England, Elizabeth I envisaged a national church and tried to include all shades of Christian opinion within the state church, by subordinating theological differences to comprehensiveness.

Toleration was, despite this, not a distinctive feature of the Anglican Church. There was constant tension between the 'Puritan' and 'Catholic' parties and both were suspicious of Roman Catholicism mainly because they saw it as part of an alliance with Spain and France to overthrow the Protestant state. However, the cause of toleration and liberty was advanced by various influences such as the philosophy of the Cambridge Platonists who maintained that revelation must be judged by reason and narrow dogmatism should be avoided. Whichcote (1609-83) wrote: 'Because I may be mistaken I must not be dogmatical. I will not break the certain laws of charity, for a doubtful doctrine or uncertain truth.' In the New World, opposition was directed against the Puritan intolerance in Massachusetts by such men as Roger Williams, who advocated civil liberty for all and defended the rights of the Indians in America; by Lord Baltimore; by the Quaker leader William Penn who maintained that liberty was a natural human right and force never made a good Christian or a good subject.

Later on John Locke (1632-1704) was to exert a marked influence in the movement towards toleration. 'Toleration,' he wrote, 'must be the chief characteristic mark of the true church. Toleration of those who disagree in religion is both agreeable to the gospel of Jesus Christ and to the genuine reason of mankind.' Thus the forces producing a general acceptance of tolerance were varied – the growth of rationalism, the rise of pacifism and opposition to force; religious indifference and opposition to established religion; the emphasis on commerce and trade which produced a more liberal and tolerant attitude in the social and political sphere – all played their part in the promotion of the idea of tolerance, leading up to the Toleration Act in England in 1689. However, the Revocation of the Edict of Nantes 1685 and the subsequent persecution of the French Huguenots and their exodus from France to England and Ireland as refugees reinforced the penal restrictions against Roman Catholics in England and Ireland which were to last until Catholic Emancipation in 1829.

In general, the mainstream of both Protestant and Catholic thought has been hostile to religious liberty. Liberty has been more often associated with non-Christian influences than with Christian. Religious enthusiasm in the case of Protestants, and religious conservatism in the case of Catholics, have produced the most extreme intolerance. Freedom and toleration have often had to rely on non-dogmatic religion, religious indifference, secular philosophy and anti-clerical politics.

Pope Gregory XVI in 1832 stated that 'from the foul well of indifferentism flows that absurd and erroneous opinion, or rather delirium, of liberty of conscience'. 'What death is worse for the soul, than the freedom to err?' Leo XIII in 1888 condemned liberty of worship as 'no liberty, but its degradation'.

In view of the traditional conservatism of the Roman Catholic Church, the teachings of Pope John XXIII and the Second Vatican Council constitute a revolution in thinking on religious liberty. In *Pacem in Terris* (1963) Pope John stated: 'Among man's rights is the right to the able to worship God in accordance with the right dictates of his own conscience and to profess his religion both in private and in public.'

The Second Vatican Council declared that 'all men are to be immune from coercion on the part of individuals or of social groups and of any human power, in such wise that no one is to be forced to act in a manner contrary to his own beliefs, whether privately or publicly, whether alone or in association with others, within due limits'. The Council further declared that 'the right to religious freedom has its foundation in the very dignity of the human person, as this dignity is known through the revealed word of God and by reason itself. In all his activity a man is bound to follow his conscience, in order that he may come to God, the end and purpose of life. It follows that he is not to be forced to act in a manner contrary to his conscience. In the life of the people of God, as it has made its pilgrim way through the vicissitudes of human history, there has at times appeared a way of acting that was hardly in accord with the spirit of the gospel, and even opposed to it.'

The aftermath of the First World War saw the disappearance of European Emperors and some monarchies with the emergence of independent nation states and emphasis on the sovereignty of the people. The example and influence of the USA gave impetus to the democratic desire to have a constitutional separation, involving the breaking of any formal or direct links between church and state. Henceforth no church or religious organisation would enjoy a privileged position. The state would have no religious favourites. This had also been the aim of Wolfe Tone and the leaders of the United Irishmen in 1798, inspired by the ideals of the French Revolution.

However, in some places the old alliance or special relationship between church and state still lingered on, for example in Franco's Spain, Salazar's Portugal and Orthodox Greece. The Church of Ireland was disestablished in 1870 and the Irish State, or Free State, came into being in 1922. At that time, the influence of the Roman Catholic Church on legislation was never seriously challenged and in De Valera's constitution of 1937 the 'special position' of the Roman Catholic Church was recognised until removed by referendum in 1975. But into the 1970s, the Roman

Catholic hierarchy was consulted by successive governments to ensure that legislation on such matters as education, the family and sexual morality would be in accordance with 'Catholic teaching' and it was customary to send messages of filial obedience to the See of Rome by the Taoiseach on behalf of the government on assuming office, e.g. De Valera and Costello. Now all has changed and the Roman Catholic Church is no longer the power in the land that it once was. Contrast the Republic today with 1949, so well portrayed in Austin Clarke's *Burial of an Irish President*, Dr Douglas Hyde's funeral service in St Patrick's Cathedral Dublin, when Costello was Taoiseach and would not, as 'a good Catholic', attend a Protestant service:

Costello, his Cabinet, in Government cars hiding
Around the corner, ready. Tall hat in hand
Dreading 'Our Father' in English. Better not hear
That 'which' for 'who' and risk eternal doom.

Protestants in 1949 said 'Our Father which art in Heaven'. Catholics said 'who'.

The Protestant Monarchy and the Orange Order
This loss of ascendancy status suffered by the Roman Catholic Church in the latter part of the twentieth century, and before that by the Church of Ireland in 1870, has helped, along with other factors like EU membership, to make the Republic a more tolerant country. It is now widely recognised that religion and politics have to commend themselves by their own integrity and not by a mutual propping up. The idea of a state established church or a confessional state, apart altogether from the scriptural and theological issues involved, is ultimately bad for both church and state. Bad for the church in that it alone is seen and held responsible for all moral defects or blemishes in society. Bad for the state in that, in an age of pluralism, religious indifference and secularism, the idea of the state upholding or giving pride of place to one particular religious denomination or interfering in religious matters, such as the appointment of bishops,

is to say the least distasteful to a growing number who have given it serious thought and many of whom are active church members. They view, for example, the establishment of the Church of England as an anachronism, the legacy of a bygone age.

Whereas in England 'the Protestant monarchy' as part of the establishment has been generally accepted without question by the majority of citizens, since it does not impinge on their daily lives nor interfere with their democratically elected parliament, in Northern Ireland it is a different story. There, especially among the 'loyal Orders', e.g. The Orange Order, Protestant monarchy and succession are taken seriously as the defenders of the Protestant faith against 'the wiles and errors of the Church of Rome'. The union centred on the Crown as Protestant Defender is seen as the guarantee of victorious Protestantism over 'treacherous and corrupt Romanism'. Hence the union flag is regarded primarily as a Protestant symbol, proudly displayed during the July marching season and announcing to all the ongoing victory over popery. This inevitably leads to Roman Catholics being seen as second class citizens, if not as traitors. Thus sectarianism in Northern Ireland is quite unwittingly boosted by the establishment of the Church of England and its Protestant succession. For 'the loyal Orders', the existence of the union without a 'Protestant' crown is a contradiction in terms. How would they react to, say, a Roman Catholic monarch and a disestablished Church of England? They certainly would lose their passion to preserve a union without a Protestant crown, but without any clear idea of what to put in its place – except perhaps to oppose a United Ireland, an opposition becoming weaker all the time as Protestant numbers and influence decline in Northern Ireland and Roman Catholic influence diminishes in the Republic.

Dedicated as it is to the political defence of the Protestant religion through the maintenance of the Protestant Crown, the Orange Order, to be true to its origin, really cannot discard its political dimension. There is the deep-rooted belief, the legacy of history, that Protestantism to survive needs the protection of the union with its Protestant monarch. All of which seems to point to a lack of faith in the ability and integrity of the reformed faith to stand on its own feet without the benefit of a political prop. The Order finds in the Old Testament – with its record of God's chosen people, the true inheritors of the promised land doing battle against heathen idolatry – a ready-to-hand analogy of the Orange Order as the one true representative of Protestant Ulster, God's chosen people, battling against papist idolatry in the cause of God and Ulster. So the Order is fervently anti-ecumenical. No joint worship or Bible study; no attendance at Roman Catholic services; no inter-church marriages with Roman Catholics; segregation, religious apartheid at official ecclesiastical levels, whatever personal relationships may exist with individual Roman Catholics. This negativism, for which the Order claims a divine sanction, is in direct conflict with forward looking ecumenical Protestantism and its belief in the ongoing guidance of the Holy Spirit to bring about mutual understanding and reconciliation and, in God's good time, unity, that 'all may be one', that 'the world may see and believe' (John 17:23). Ecumenism helps to correct what has been amiss and to supply what is lacking in our common Christian witness and presents the Orange Order with a choice between a Protestantism which looks to the future and is prepared 'to launch out into the deep', as the disciples did at the command of Jesus (Luke 5:5), or to remain firmly shackled to the past. It should be made abundantly clear that the anti-ecumenism of the Orange Order is contrary to the witness and practice of the Church of Ireland today. The Church of Ireland is committed to ecumenism at all levels, parish, diocesan, national and international. We have thankfully moved out of the confrontational mind-set of the seventeenth century.

Both the Orange Order and their republican opponents, for example on the Garvaghy Road, Portadown, use religion for party political ends, Protestant 'rights' against Catholic 'sensitivities'. The Orange Order wraps the Bible in the union flag and the republicans wrap the crucifix in the Irish tricolour. In so doing both are demeaning their religion and their politics. Sheer sectarian confrontation under the guise of Christianity has taken the place of the Christian gospel of love, generosity and humility. Sadly the Christian churches at the outset of the troubles, instead of, like the prophets of old, courageously proclaiming to all and sundry that what was being done in the name of Protestantism or Roman Catholicism was a travesty of the Christian gospel, have instead too often sought to explain or excuse or justify the unChristian actions of their respective adherents by reference to past events and 'battles long ago', 'This is very unfortunate but …'.

Christianity is here not to excuse the past but to change the present.

The turn-off point in religion for many young and old is when they see the institutional churches accommodating attitudes and actions grounded in the past which are a flagrant denial of the teaching of Jesus. They lose touch with the churches when the churches lose touch with Jesus. They may have rejected the churches but not Jesus. For example, the spectacle of Orange confrontation at Drumcree, paralleled by nationalist intransigence on the Garvaghy Road. Where is Jesus and the generosity of the gospel in all this vitriolic and aggressive self-righteousness? Why cannot one side or the other relinquish their so called 'rights' as Jesus would have done, indeed did so, when refused right of passage through Samaria? In doing so, not only would they follow Jesus and the gospel, but would take the moral high ground and gain national and international approval.

In a conflict situation, those who, like the Orange Order, refuse to talk directly without preconditions to their opponents, while at the same time self righteously condemning other loyal Orders for doing so, should have been told publicly, loud and clear, by the Protestant church authorities that by their refusal to talk they were acting contrary to the gospel imperative and the example of Our Lord himself. Worship with such an attitude of intransigence and self righteousness smacks more of the making of a political statement than of commitment to the gospel – politicised religion masquerading as Christianity.

Generosity is at the heart of the gospel but what we have, so evident in Drumcree, is the prostitution of the gospel in the interests of party politics and religious sectarianism, sadly for years not only condoned but accommodated by the institutional churches.

And Drumcree didn't happen yesterday. Over the past four or five years, instead of the churches' outright condemnation of this travesty of the gospel enacted annually, we have witnessed attempts to placate, to keep the protagonists on board, and at times even to praise them for their restraint. Instead of hearing the gospel imperative, 'Thus saith the Lord' loud and clear, participants have seen the churches' attitude, if not exactly favourable, at least neutral. Only in 1999 in the Church of Ireland were certain positive and laudable resolutions passed by the General Synod to deal with such issues as Drumcree and the Orange Order. However, no firm action was taken towards their implementation, and silence to avoid controversy seems to have been the rule of the General Synod meeting in Belfast in May 2000 and in Dublin 2001. Those who turned a blind eye to the resolutions of their General Synod were not reprimanded or called to account.

What a wonderful witness for real Christianity – not the watered down political variety – if both Archbishops of Armagh had, at the outset, descended on their respective co-religionists at Drumcree and Garvaghy and from their pulpits spelt out clearly, concisely and courageously the demands of the gospel and its total condemnation of those who, while professing to follow Christ and his teaching, blatantly oppose it by their words and actions, thereby 'crucifying Christ afresh'. (Hebrews 6:6) Like the prophets of old, resolved to speak the word of God, to lay the gospel teaching 'on the line', whatever the consequences – 'whether they will hear or stop their ears'. (Ezekial 2:7)

Instead the picture has been of some church leaders working night and day to try and achieve some political fix to satisfy the warring parties while at the same time leaving them without any sense of guilt or need of repentance, with their pride and self-righteousness intact. One wonders if the leadership really believe the church to be a divine society against which ultimately the gates of hell cannot prevail, or primarily, if not solely, a political party with a religious veneer in which, to avoid splits and keep everyone on board, gospel imperatives are abandoned or take second place.

The presence of the Church of Ireland Archbishop of Armagh in the Drumcree pulpit, and in Ardoyne accompanied by the other Protestant church leaders escorting Roman Catholic children to their school (whatever the legitimate grievances of the Protestants in Ardoyne), would have done more for the Christian witness of the Church of Ireland and the Protestant community than all the sweeping condemnations of the behaviour of so-called loyalists and Protestants emanating from an episcopal residence. Archbishop Desmond Tutu in similar situations would have been out there in the thick of it all, on the ground, giving a Christian lead – as indeed he has done on a visit to Belfast with not a Church of Ireland bishop in sight.

In truth, the churches have been in hock to party political expediency. The policy has been to keep everyone happy and the congregation intact and if that means taking care not to do or say anything which might offend the anti-ecumenical sectarian segregationists or political activists, so be it. Stick to vague generalities; preach love in the abstract; avoid its application to the particular; reduce religion to the personal level of individual salvation (my personal Saviour) or to a mechanical ritual isolated from what one may think or do in the social or political field; side step the challenge of the Cross, go along with the political status quo for a quiet life, and trust that somehow we can have a resurrection without a crucifixion, an Easter without a Good Friday. So we settle for an emasculated party political Christianity which in the end brings nothing but dishonour and discredit on this island of saints and scholars and crucifies Christ afresh, putting him to an open shame. (Hebrews 6:6) Priority is given to the survival of the institution instead of to the challenge of the gospel.

We still suffer from Constantine's establishing of the Christian Church as the official religion of the Empire in the fourth century. From that time the success of Christianity has been measured by worldly standards, size, quantity, number. Greater numbers mean greater power and influence in a worldly, though not necessarily in a spiritual sense. The New Testament talks of the 'little flock', the little leaven, the pinch of salt (Luke 12:32), as the means whereby God's purpose is achieved, not by the big battalions or way of the world. All churches in a materialistic age and climate will lose out numerically, to indifference, agnosticism, atheism, esoteric sects, fanaticism and so forth. But God will never leave himself without witness. What will emerge will be slimmer, fitter, more committed to the Christian calling.

The Orange Order is really the last bastion of White, Anglo-Saxon Protestantism or WASP in the United Kingdom. Britain is becoming more multi-racial, multi-cultural and multi-religious along with prevailing secularism and indifference to all religion. Unionist loyalty as evinced by the Orange Order is to a monolithic White Anglo-Saxon Protestant monarchical British State, a relic of the seventeenth century, no longer relevant or realistic in the twenty-first century. The official link of the Ulster Unionist Party with the Orange Order alienates Roman Catholics, and adds to the perception of unionism as exclusively Protestant, Roman Catholics not welcome, to the detriment of unionism.

In Northern Ireland the Protestant population is becoming increasingly middle aged and elderly. Protestant children and youth are thin on the ground compared to Roman Catholics. Emigration, smaller families, a sense of insecurity and uncertainty about the future have taken their toll. Streets and housing estates once solidly Protestant are now Roman Catholic. New houses in great numbers and price ranges are being built all over the province, many of which are taken up by a growing self confident youthful Roman Catholic population. So Protestantism/ unionism is faced with the prospect of a Roman Catholic majority within the next 15 or 20 or less years, and also the prospect of devolution in Scotland and Wales, especially Scotland, leading to the fragmentation of the United Kingdom as we know it. Unionism, beset with bitter internecine strife, has no plans to cope with such an eventuality and the Protestant churches have so identified themselves with unionism and the religious dimension of the British Establishment that they will promptly be dismissed by the Roman Catholic majority as irrelevant theologically as well as politically. Protestantism will not be taken seriously by the Roman Catholic majority as an expression of the gospel, but brushed aside as a pseudo religious and political anachronism. The broad identity of Roman Catholicism with the successful nationalist opponents of unionism will ensure that the Roman Catholic Church in the short term will fare better, but in the longer term, as memories of past injustices fade and secularism, scepticism and religious indifference take their toll, the influence of the Roman Catholic Church in Northern Ireland will surely diminish as in the Republic.

The disestablishment of the Church of Ireland in 1870 was strenuously opposed by the Irish bishops in the House of Lords as later on was the proposal to grant Home Rule. The Church of Ireland, deprived of its voice in the House of Lords, feared that severance or weakening of the union would be detrimental, if not indeed fatal, for the future of Protestantism in Ireland as a minority religion in a Roman Catholic state. The church identified itself very much with the British presence and accordingly looked on Protestant Home Rulers as misguided romantics or troublemakers, certainly not in accordance with the convictions of the vast majority of Church of Ireland members. The landed gentry and leading members of the legal profession involved in the British administration held a paramount influence in church synods in articulating the opposition to Home Rule. In the North, the Solemn League and Covenant organised by Carson, with its threat 'to use all means found necessary to defeat the present conspiracy to set up a Home Rule Parliament in Ireland', while not receiving official synodical support nevertheless received widespread acclaim in the Church of Ireland, inasmuch as those who refused to sign, for example Bishop Chadwick of

Derry, found themselves in a tiny and unpopular minority within the church.

The Church of Ireland landlords and their allies in the professions, who played a leading role in church synods and councils, saw the union as crucial if they were to maintain that exalted political and social status to which they had grown accustomed. They also saw the union as essential to the very existence of Protestantism in Ireland, as they understood it, more Anglo than Irish, superior to the superstitious 'candles of the Irish poor', while, as in Louis McNiece's Carrickfergus, 'The Chichesters knelt in marble at the end of the transept with ruffs about their necks, their portion sure'. It should however be noted that the ordinary Protestant farmers, shopkeepers or tradesmen were never treated as equals by the landowning aristocracy, never invited to social events arranged by the 'big house' such as dinner parties or shooting parties, and never addressed by using the intimacy of a Christian name, always the surname, Griffin, Jackson, Molloy etc, to remind them of their deferential state. No special favour was bestowed on the Protestants. Know your place. Respect your 'betters'. Mrs C. F. Alexander, the great hymn writer, had no difficulty in accepting the 'divinely ordained' social order when she wrote: 'The rich man in his castle, the poor man at the gate, God made them high and lowly and ordered their estate.' At the same time fears, real or imagined, for their very existence as Protestants under Home Rule percolated down from church synods and councils and alienated Protestants, with a few honourable exceptions, from playing a constructive part in endeavouring to achieve a Home Rule arrangement, non-sectarian and inclusive. So for Protestants in general, Home Rule became synonymous with Rome Rule and unionism indispensable, not only to the survival of the 'big house', but to the survival of their religion in Ireland. With the end of unionism and the decline of the 'big house', especially in the twenty six counties, Protestantism allied to unionism was inevitably regarded by the majority as a foreign anti-Irish religion and suffered accordingly, rapidly declining in numbers and influence. A sombre warning here for Protestantism in Northern Ireland today.

In the years following disestablishment, the Church of Ireland, as well as being concerned with the Home Rule question, had also to deal with crucial internal matters: how to adjust to the new situation, not only in matters of liturgy and canonical regulations but also church finance and property, in a word, to produce a new constitution for a new role as the same Church of Ireland but no longer enjoying a preferential and privileged position in the state. Due to the loyalty and devotion and expertise of its leaders, clerical and lay, this was successfully and speedily accomplished, with the Church of Ireland becoming autonomous and its General Synod, consisting of the bishops, elected clergy and laity, as the parliament of the church and ultimate authority under God.

The Easter rebellion of 1916 was totally abhorrent to the majority of Church of Ireland people – and for many others also – a stab in the back for Britain who was fighting with many loyal Irish in the ranks to save Europe from enslavement to a tyrannical Kaiser. The battle of the Somme which also occurred in the same year was, and is still, firmly embedded in the psyche of the Ulster Protestant people. There is the conviction that the dissolving of the union would be a betrayal of their gallant dead who made the supreme sacrifice in the horrific trench battles of the Great War. Church of Ireland and all Protestant churches (and some Roman Catholic), not only in Ulster but throughout the country, mourned the dead in yearly Remembrance or Armistice Day services and honoured the King under whose banner they had fought and died.

The Great War had a significant impact on the minority Church of Ireland population in the south of Ireland which sustained a heavy loss in proportion to their number. Many sons and heirs were killed. There was a feeling of uncertainty and vulnerability made more acute by the spectacle of the Easter rebellion and its aftermath. Many decided to pack up and leave the country and this fear of what the future might hold for them was heightened by the burning of Protestant houses, usually but not always the 'big house' of the landlord, the murder of policemen and innocent Protestants, such as in west Cork, by republicans. All this prompted the General Synod to send representatives led by Archbishop Gregg of Dublin to the Sinn Féin Provisional Government, represented by Michael Collins and William Cosgrave, to ask that the Church of Ireland population 'be made secure in the elementary rights of citizens of a Christian country and to seek to allay their fears'. The archbishop in his diary mentions the outcome as 'satisfactory' but gives no details of what transpired. There was disappointment at the failure of the Irish representatives to consult with the authorities of the Church of Ireland on the drawing up of the Treaty which brought into being the new Irish Free State, although Archbishop Gregg of Dublin, who had previously criticised the exclusion of Protestants from any input, stated that 'the new constitution will claim our allegiance with the same solemn authority as the one that is now being constitutionally annulled'. The Irish Free State came into being on 6 December 1922 and, while the Church of Ireland and Protestants as a whole thought the severance of the link with Britain and the resultant partition of Ireland a disaster of great magnitude, nevertheless the Church of Ireland through its synods, councils, and bishops pledged full support, loyalty and goodwill towards the new state and hoped that 'its members would be enabled to play a constructive part in its affairs'. Contrast this with the refusal of the Roman Catholic hierarchy in Northern Ireland to recognise or co-operate with the new Northern Ireland state, leading to a unionist suspicion that all Roman Catholics were enemies of the state and hence could not be trusted. Discrimination was therefore inevitable. De Valera, in drawing up his Constitution of 1937 to replace the 1922 Constitution, was very anxious that all articles would be agreeable to Roman Catholic teaching on faith and morals and to ensure this he had consultations with Roman Catholic authorities at the highest Vatican level. But he did not consult the other churches, except to ask Archbishop Gregg's advice on the correct titles to be used for the churches specified in the Constitution. The Church of Ireland accepted this Constitution without, at any rate publicly or officially, raising any objection to any article. There was the silence of submission dictated no doubt by fear of what might befall the minority Church of Ireland community being perceived as opponents of the state.

The war years (1939-45) saw a trickle of Church of Ireland men joining the Irish army and local defence and security forces, but many more opting for the British forces and active particip- ation in a war in which Éire was neutral. There was no doubt where Church of Ireland and Protestant sympathies lay and great rejoicing erupted on VE day in Dublin which was met by energetic anti-British demonstrations by republicans. During the immediate post war years, right up to the civil rights move- ment, the majority of Church of Ireland people in the Republic as it had now become, envied their co-religionists in the North and the benefits which they enjoyed as citizens of the United Kingdom. As Church of Ireland members living in a state with a Roman Catholic ethos and in moral questions controlled by the Church of Rome, they had little or no sympathy with voices raised against the alleged misdeeds of the northern unionist ad- ministration and the vitriolic attacks by republicans on Britain and the northern Protestants.

The general attitude was, 'We as Protestants have to put up with all sorts of things we dislike down here in the Republic, boycotts as in Fetherd on Sea in Co Wexford, job discrimination, compulsory Irish, Roman Catholic canon law upheld by the state, the *Ne Temere* marriage decree (which contributed in no small measure to a decrease in the Protestant population in the Republic from 10 percent in 1920 to little over 3 percent in 1990, whereas in Northern Ireland the Roman Catholic population in- creased by 10 percent over the same period); a 1937 Constitution reflecting Roman Catholic values, etc. So what have the Roman Catholics in Northern Ireland to whinge about, especially since they are enjoying all the educational, health and welfare benefits of the United Kingdom, far in excess of anything here in the Republic?'

There was the accepted and general connotation that the authentic Irish person was a Roman Catholic, anti-British nationalist, and supporter of all things Gaelic – in that order. This was reinforced by both DeValera and Costello sending messages of allegiance to the Pope on behalf of the Irish government and people, and by the fact that such republican activists as Maud Gonne, Casement, and Countess Markievicz converted to Roman Catholicism. This left the Irish Protestants, and especially the Northern Ireland Protestant unionists in a sort of limbo. 'If that's Irish, then count me out. I'm not Irish, I'm British.' Before partition, identity was never a problem for the Irish Protestant, North or South. Irish Protestant unionists like Carson had no difficulty in being Irish *and* British, in that order; there was no contradiction.

Before partition the Protestants saw themselves as Irish who valued and sought to maintain the link with the neighbouring island, believing that the two islands formed a natural geographic and economic unity which must not be broken by the partition of the United Kingdom; a United Ireland as part of a United Kingdom. In the end, what we got was not only the partition of the United Kingdom, but the partition of Ireland as well which no-one really wanted, least of all Carson.

Both the Church of Ireland/unionists and the Roman Catholic/nationalists were opposed to the partition of Ireland but for different reasons. Partition for one meant partitioning the United Kingdom with the southern Irish unionists, an alienated minority cut off from the Westminster Parliament and ruled instead by a nationalist/Roman Catholic Dublin parliament where Home Rule would become Rome Rule, and also depriving them of the support of their northern co-religionists. Partition for the other, the Roman Catholic nationalists, meant the mutilation of the 32 county Irish nation with the nationalist/Roman Catholic northern minority ruled by a Protestant/ unionist dominated Stormont parliament, and also depriving them of the support of their southern co-religionists. Whereas the Irish unionists looked on the two islands together as the natural political and geographic unity from which a minority in the twenty six counties had no democratic right to secede, the Irish nationalists looked on the island of Ireland as the natural political and geographic unity from which a minority in the six counties had no democratic right to secede.

So southern Protestants, a small minority, isolated from their northern co-religionists, living in a state which extolled its Catholicism and nationalism as essentials of 'Irishness', the southern Protestants, for the most part – there were a few exceptions such as W. B. Yeats – kept their heads down, a low profile, lest they should be accused of ill will towards the new state. I well remember my mother's warning: 'Keep off religion and politics or you'll get us all burnt out.' How often have I heard southern Protestant ex-unionists saying, 'The British left when it suited them and left us high and dry.' Here the Hubert Butler case is significant.

Hubert Butler was censured by local government bodies, expelled from committees, forced to resign from the Kilkenny Archaeological Society which he had founded, because in the interest of historical accuracy he had dared to mention at a meeting in Dublin in 1952 the forced conversion of 240,000 Orthodox Serbs to Roman Catholicism in Croatia under the dictator Pavelitch during the Hitlerite period.

The Papal Nuncio, of whose presence Butler was unaware, walked out, and accusations resounded throughout the land that Hubert Butler had insulted the Papal Nuncio. In truth he had insulted no one and never intended to do so. He attempted to make a well-informed contribution – for he knew Yugoslavia well – and to give a balanced view of the situation in Croatia under Hitler's puppet, Pavelitch, in 1941. There was no upsurge of Protestant support for Hubert Butler. Protestants were scared. Which tells us something about Protestants but also something about the Roman Catholic community at that time. Had Protestants good reason to be scared? Looking at what happened to Hubert Butler, perhaps they had. I can hear again my mother's warning: 'Keep quiet Victor, or you'll get us all burnt out!'

I was a curate in Derry in 1952 and wrote to Hubert Butler offering my sympathy and support. Many years later when I returned to Dublin we met and lunched together and thereafter he wrote to me frequently, expressing approval of what I was saying about the need for a pluralist society. He believed, as I do, that the Irish at heart, both Catholic and Protestant, are a tolerant people. They are made intolerant by tribal religion masquerading as Christianity.

Outwardly Protestants, keeping their fears and misgivings to themselves, appeared contented, finding no fault in public with their new rulers. This was understandable but it gave the wrong signal to the majority community, especially to those of the extreme republican tradition. Since, they argued, 'the Protestants in the south appear quite satisfied to live under a Dublin government, why can't the northern Protestants adopt a similar attitude?'

It can't have anything to do with their Protestantism since their co-religionists in the twenty six counties seem happy enough. Therefore, it must be something else which is keeping the northern Protestants from joining in a United Ireland. What is it? Why, of course, the *Brits*. Therefore 'Brits out' and all will be well. Hence the Provos war cry – utterly simplistic and unrealistic, accusing Britain of using the northern unionists for her imperialist purposes and ignoring the crucial fact that the Brits include the Northern Ireland Protestants.

Partition left the southern Protestants alienated, isolated, an insecure and uncertain minority confronted by the might of an authoritarian and unchallenged Roman Catholic Church and a submissive state; an alliance which ultimately has proved detrimental to both church and state, with painful consequences in the moral and legal spheres and the reputation and credibility of church and state severely tarnished.

Partition gave rise to a siege mentality amongst the majority northern Protestant unionist community whose fear of absorption into a Roman Catholic dominated Republic inevitably led to discrimination, for example in jobs and housing, against the minority Roman Catholic nationalists who were regarded as traitors to the state, bent on undermining the union, etc. With the advent of TV and the civil rights movement, unionists on the international scene have fared very badly, being perceived as the oppressors of a downtrodden and embittered Catholic minority. Unionists were very slow in coming to terms with the power of the media, resentful of its intrusion, while nationalists welcomed and used it to full advantage, never slow to emphasise, even exaggerate, defects and injustices, often giving the impression that they lived disenfranchised in a fascist state. The message went out that unionists were solely to blame always for everything everywhere. Contrast the sympathetic treatment of the nationalist/Catholic community in films such as 'Bloody Sunday' and 'In The Name of the Father' with the absence of anything similar on the Enniskillen Remembrance Sunday and other multiple murders of Protestants by the IRA. The unionists blame the media but in truth over the years they have been reluctant to embrace it and so have allowed their case to go by default. Even when dealt a hand of trumps they have somehow managed to lose every trick. Partition has left us a legacy of psychological and physical Protestant and Roman Catholic mutually suspicious ghettos throughout Northern Ireland. While partition may well have been inevitable in the prevailing circumstances of that time, it has copperfastened sectarian religious and political tribalism in which all are losers, unionist and nationalist, Protestant and Roman Catholic, North and South.

'Thank God, we are not like the others.' Really? I wonder 'if the boot had been on the other foot' would the situation have been any different? Imagine in the Republic a growing unionist and Protestant minority approaching 40 per cent, parading their union flags, singing 'God Save the Queen', advocating union with Britain. Would such a minority, threatening the very existence of the Republic, seen as traitors to the state, have been treated better at the hands of the nationalist majority in the Republic than the nationalist minority at the hands of the Unionists in

Northern Ireland? I don't think so. All majorities, when they feel threatened, will take what they regard as necessary measures, however unpleasant and unjust, to stem the rising tide. This is the way things are and the pot should beware of calling the kettle black.

Irish Protestants and Partition

Irish Protestants, it now seems, would have fared much better in a united Ireland. There, as a significant minority with increased numerical strength and influence and the support of liberal Catholics and others, they would have presented a serious challenge to the dominance of the Roman Catholic Church in political affairs, thereby giving a lead to many liberal Roman Catholics and others who were unhappy with the Roman Catholic ethos of the state and who wished for a more pluralist, tolerant and open society. As an integral part, and fully supportive of the state, Irish Protestantism would have received more respect and favourable attention from the Irish people as a whole, than at present enjoyed by the northern Protestants among the people of the United Kingdom, for many of whom, perhaps a majority, they are an enigma and embarrassment. The UK would shed few tears at the departure of Northern Ireland.

A united Ireland would also have presented the Protestants with the opportunity to promote a close association and special relationship with the neighbouring island, so helping to heal the centuries of strife and bitterness and perhaps discovering in the process, a new and enriched concept of unionism.

For the Protestants in the Irish Free State, as it then was, after partition further decline was inevitable. A tiny beleaguered submissive minority was confronted with the might of an authoritarian Roman Catholic Church allied to a compliant deferential state. On the other hand, the northern Protestants were confronted by a substantial and growing Roman Catholic and nationalist community who denied the legitimacy of the northern state in spite of enjoying all its UK benefits, and who had the support of successive Dublin governments. Accordingly the northern Protestants were driven into a defensive 'no surrender' siege mentality and were widely depicted on the international scene by polemical anti-partition Dublin voices as the oppressors of a downtrodden Roman Catholic community.

All have lost from the partition of Ireland but the Protestants have lost the most of all.

Partition also placed the RUC in a 'no-win' situation, especially since the Roman Catholic Church, following the nationalist lead, would not recognise the Northern Ireland state or encourage its members to participate. Hence a blanket condemnation of the RUC as a sectarian force was inevitable, its misdeeds and shortcomings loudly trumpeted, but its day to day service to the whole community and its commendable restraint in spite of cold blooded murder, mutilation and bitter provocation from all sides, largely unrecognised, unhonoured and unsung in the nationalist community. Would any police force, anywhere in the world, have behaved any better in such circumstances or indeed as well as the RUC?

At the outset, partition was looked on only as a temporary arrangement. Today many unionists are saying in private that in the context of the European Union, the prosperity and plurality of the Irish Republic, demographic changes unfavourable to unionism, devolution in Scotland and Wales, a united Ireland is inevitable within the next twenty years or so. And there is the widespread realisation that the British would be very happy to be rid of Northern Ireland. There are unionists, albeit a small minority, who believe that their best interests would be served by doing a deal with the Republic while they still have bargaining power and agree on some form of a united Ireland, federal or otherwise, in which 'unionism' would have greater influence than it ever would in the United Kingdom.

This unholy mixture of religion and party politics for centuries has been the curse of Ireland. Christianity has always been the loser. Christianity, whatever its denominational character, if it is to be true to its founder, must make its own way and commend itself by its own integrity. It needs no political props. All it should require of the state is freedom to preach and practise its faith and disciplines within the context of an agreed public order and morality. Too often Protestantism is perceived as the unionists or West Brits at prayer, as the religious dimension of unionism; and Roman Catholicism as the nationalists at prayer, the religious dimension of Nationalism. Christianity has been debased by party political entanglements, and politics has also been demeaned by sectarian or confessional influences. Whereas in Northern Ireland politics has dominated religion, in the Republic religion has, at least until the 1980s, dominated politics. Failure of the churches in Northern Ireland to challenge the political status quo was matched by failure of the politicians in the Republic, with one or two honourable exceptions such as Dr Noel Browne, to challenge the dominance of the Roman Catholic Church.

This means that neither Protestantism nor Catholicism has been judged on its merits as an expression of the gospel of Christ but was so often, by so many, seen and evaluated in a political context, and the political ingredient has resulted in a more conservative and diehard Roman Catholicism and Protestantism in Northern Ireland, holding fast to the old ways, nervous of change for fear of letting the side down. As Christians, especially in Ireland today, of all denominations, we must firmly reject any political stranglehold on religion and any religious stranglehold on politics in which both are losers, leaving a legacy of cynicism and disillusionment. And we must emphasis that Irishness transcends religion and politics, is inclusive and is best defined as a sense of place, of belonging, of home in a common homeland.

Look at the title, Church of Ireland. Is it not somewhat arrogant for a church with only seventeen percent of the population in Northern Ireland and, say, three percent in the Republic to claim to be the Church of Ireland? Merely on numerical grounds there can be no justification whatsoever for such a claim, which can be dismissed as a relic of the British political and religious establishment. But there may be some justification in that, though in a minority numerically, the Church of Ireland in its

membership covers the whole spectrum of Irish political opinion from republicanism to unionism, perhaps to an extent not
equalled by any other denomination in Ireland; an all-Ireland
church with an all-Ireland political inclusion and with its head-
quarters in Dublin. In General Synod, Cork republicans sit
alongside Antrim unionists. Therefore to be true to its name and
claim, the Church of Ireland, especially in Northern Ireland, in
its leadership should be very careful to avoid any action or policy
which would lend support to the view that the Church of
Ireland is primarily, if not solely, the religious dimension of
unionism and the British establishment. It is embarrassing to
many loyal and thoughtful Church of Ireland members to have
their Primate of All Ireland, the Archbishop of Armagh, sitting
in the House of Lords while still in office, thereby identifying the
whole Church of Ireland, north and south, albeit unintentionally,
with the British establishment.

For 300 years, the Church of Ireland was looked on as the
arm of the British ascendancy in Ireland and was not taken seriously in matters of theology or ethics. It was dismissed out of
hand as simply the lapdog of the British. Only now in the
Republic, freed from the stigma of British ascendancy, is the
Church of Ireland and Protestantism in general, being judged on
its merits as an expression of the gospel, making a contribution
in many spheres which is welcomed by the community at large
in a state which has become more open, tolerant, pluralist during the past twenty five years. Indeed, the civil rights movement
in the north prompted many in the Republic of all religions or
none, who were dissatisfied with the confessional ethos of the
state, to advocate in public what they had previously felt in private, with the result that pressure for change built up. Gone are
the days when government ministers, hat in hand, waited on the
approval of the Roman Catholic Archbishop of Dublin, John
Charles McQuaid, for any suggested legislation involving what
the church regarded as a moral issue in such spheres as welfare,
health and education. Indeed, during direct rule the Roman
Catholic Church had more influence with the British adminis-

tration in Northern Ireland than with the Irish government in
the Republic, especially on financial grants for their schools.

Morality and the Constitution in a Democratic State
While there are different types of 'society' there is nevertheless a
large measure of agreement on certain laws, regarded as basic to
any society and finding universal acceptance. Any civilised
form of social life requires that there should be rules governing
the relations between persons in regard to such matters as respect for life and property, return for services rendered, sexual
relationships, etc, and that they should be generally obeyed.
And the rules and obligations are in a general way such obvious
conditions of individual and social well-being that most of them
are included in the moral code of most peoples. Social life would
be impossible without legal prohibition against, for example,
murder, stealing, etc.

Thus there is a common or public morality, recognised and
enforced in all societies. This, however, does not constitute the
entire morality of any society. For example, the morality of western society has been largely determined by Jewish and Christian
influence. It is thus part of public morality in Christian society
that, for example, polygamy is illegal and that women have certain fundamental rights and a higher status than is accorded to
them in some non-Christian societies. Social morality is not the
result of pure reasoning or logical inference in a vacuum. It is
fashioned by the various influences, cultural, religious and economic, which are or have been present in the society.

While there is a large measure of agreement amongst
Christians on many matters of social or 'public' morality, there
is also an area of disagreement. Controversial matters include
such questions as contraception, abortion, sterilisation, divorce,
homosexuality. Those who argue for a total prohibition by society, through its legislature or constitution, of these practices
sometimes do so on the grounds that there is an overriding
moral authority with the wisdom to know and the responsibility
to inform society that such things are morally wrong, or contrary to the will of God for the moral ordering of society.

At times such authority has felt that it had a right and a duty to exert pressure on the state and to control legislation involving moral issues. Nor has such 'final arbiter or authority' always been ecclesiastical or theological. Plato in his *Republic* treats the rulers or 'philosopher-kings' as infallible, having the right to impose strict control on the thoughts and behaviour of the citizens. For Plato there is no intrinsic value in the idea of freedom of thought or action. Thus, 'final authority' or authoritarianism whether in an ecclesiastical, political or philosophical form, has been a recurring feature of morality at certain periods. Morality is absolute and objective. It is known in a Platonic sense to a ruling elite who have discovered it by an infallible logical process and who have the right and duty to impose it on society. It is known in the ecclesiastical sense to a clerical hierarchy to whom has been given by God the gift of moral discernment and certainty, with the sanction to endeavour to impose such moral teaching on society for its own good.

Any society pledged to uphold democracy and freedom must be prepared to tolerate different views and practices in relation to certain moral questions. It must avoid being morally legalistic, enforcing a particular view through its constitution, legislature and courts in matters of controversy over deeply and sincerely held convictions in the moral sphere. It may be described as a pluralist society. A pluralist society, however, does not abstain from making public moral judgments or enforcing certain moral principles. No society can discard its general moral ethos which has been fashioned by various influences, and the moral attitudes of any society are naturally reflected in its concept and implementation of its social or public morality. On the other hand, for legislators merely to reflect the majority opinion can be dangerous. Majority opinion in Tzarist Russia was certainly anti-semitic, and in Hitlerite Germany the policy of anti-semitism may well have had majority support, for educational, political and racial brainwashing can bend the minds of citizens to suit their political or religious rulers. While legislators should always be concerned with prohibiting what is likely to corrupt society, yet they should be continually on their guard against organisations or pressure groups who predict social degeneration and decay, not on empirical and factual evidence but on some prior theological, political or racist convictions. Unless there is clear, unmistakable factual evidence that any controversial matter, such as contraception, divorce or abortion, would never under any circumstances substantially reduce human suffering and injustice but would on the contrary always be a detrimental and corrupting influence on the quality of life in society, the state should refrain from prohibitory legislation while at the same time taking all reasonable steps in safeguarding society against abuses or permissiveness.

By public morality we mean the morality of acts whose performance is properly a matter for the judgement of society, either because such acts are performed in public or are capable of having a direct influence on the public.

By private morality we mean the morality of acts whose performance is solely a matter of private judgement since such acts are always performed in private and are not capable of having a direct influence on the public.

Although it is evident that a clear line cannot be drawn between public and private morality, the onus rests on those who would interfere with private moral judgements and conduct, to show in an unmistakable way by the use of all available relevant factual and scientific information that what they intend to prohibit is detrimental to society. There must be a clear and well attested case for interfering with the liberty and freedom of conscience of individuals. Privacy must be respected and if there is any reasonable doubt the law must come down on the side of privacy and freedom of conscience (always of course recognising that such freedom of conscience and action does not conflict with the code of public morality which has general acceptance).

Laws should command the respect of reasonable people. They must be credible and not be offensive to common sense. For example, any law which would equate the use of certain contraceptive devices with murder on the grounds that they are 'abortifacients' and that 'all abortion is murder' is clearly repugnant to the common sense of a great number of people. Laws should not be enacted which are likely to produce a great deal of suffering for some people or to give encouragement to such practices as blackmail. For example, the complete prohibition of divorce or abortion under all circumstances may result in causing intense suffering which society has no right to inflict and such total and absolute prohibition is an offence against Christian compassion and concern.

There are some actions which are always morally wrong under normal conditions. But that does not rule out the possibility that in highly exceptional circumstances such actions may be morally justifiable. Under normal conditions such behaviour would always be morally wrong, but moral rules are intended to operate against a background of normality, not in conditions which confront us with agonising choices. Ultimately, the well-being of the individual person is all important and that person is deserving always of Christian compassion and concern.

For example the restrictive laws in the Irish Republic in the 1980s, limiting the obtaining of contraceptives to married couples on a doctor's prescription, was an unwarranted invasion of privacy, and theological rectitude takes precedence whenever and wherever the use of condoms for the prevention or alleviation of suffering to those at risk from HIV or AIDS, especially in Africa, is forbidden on absolutist moral grounds.

The mark of a 'free' or pluralist society is not that it abstains from making moral judgments or enforcing certain moral principles, but that it is prepared to submit its proposed or actual moral leglislation to the most rigorous scientific and informed examination; it must be continually 'open' to serious and constructive views from whatever quarter they may come and must have a willingness to change laws if necessary in the light of experience and reasonable public opinion. A pluralist society will be sceptical of authoritarianism or 'pressure groups', whether ecclesiastical, political or racial, and will keep its legislation on moral matters to a minimum.

Within the basic framework of public morality on which there is a general consensus and agreement, each church must have the right to preach and practise its own faith and moral disciplines and to offer guidance to its members.

The state must not take sides and in a morally controversial issue enforce a particular moral view, even a majority one, on all its citizens. The sole function of the state must be to ensure freedom for all within the context of a generally agreed and accepted public order and morality. The measure of democracy is shown in its treatment of minorities. It follows that complex moral issues, in which there are sincerely held but different points of view or shades of opinion, should not be the subject of constitutional definition or decree. In a pluralist state a Constitution should express a general consensus, setting out basic human rights and responsibilities, and steering clear of controversial and divisive moral issues. Such issues should be the affair not of the Constitution but of the legislature, always bearing in mind that each church must have the right to exercise its own particular moral disciplines and none the right to enforce them on others. Only in this way will we ensure in our democratic societies that the church does not usurp the functions of the state and state does not frustrate the role of the church. In this way we shall seek to keep a sense of proportion and obey the precept of Our Lord, 'to render unto Caesar the things which are Caesar's and unto God the things that are God's.'

CHAPTER 3

Ecumenism: A Bridge Too Far?

The Papacy
'Thou art Peter and upon this rock I will build my church.' (Matthew 16:18, 19)
'When thou art converted, strengthen thy brethren.' (Luke 22:31, 32)
'Feed my sheep.' (John 21:15-17)

Until the fourth century such texts, the Petrine texts, were taken as referring to Peter personally without any reference to the Church of Rome, and amongst the earliest Christian fathers and teachers there was a difference of opinion as to what exactly Our Lord meant by 'this rock'. Was the rock Peter, or Christ himself, or the faith which Peter confessed?

Nowhere was infallibility inferred from the text. Indeed Peter from the record of scripture was certainly not infallible 'in matters of faith and morals', e.g. Matthew 16:22, Galatians 2:11. Irenaeus, writing at the end of the second century, speaks of 'the blessed apostles Peter and Paul having founded and built the church in Rome'. Both apostles are given the honour. Paul wrote the Epistle to the Romans and spoke of himself as having 'the care of all the churches'. So if we call an apostle like Peter or Paul a bishop, because he exercised episcopal functions as a bishop does today, we must conclude that a bishop might hold several sees, the care of many churches at once, so the Church of Rome would not have had an exclusive claim to Peter or Paul. Antioch or Jerusalem could also on the same principle lay claim to Peter as indeed they do in the Eastern Orthodox tradition.

Nevertheless, the fact that Peter was in Rome with Paul and that he was chosen and given by Our Lord himself a position of leadership in the apostolic body would naturally lead to Peter being regarded as bishop or leader of the Church of Rome.

Christians are generally agreed on this. Disagreement arises with the claim that the role of Peter would have involved universal jurisdiction or the ordering of the affairs of local or national churches, or the claim to infallibility and that such alleged prerogatives were passed on to all the bishops of Rome as successors to Peter.

Whatever form Christian unity eventually takes, I believe a reformed, less centralised papacy will have a leading role. The Bishop of Rome, on historical grounds alone, has a rightful claim to be regarded as universal primate and pastor, as a focus of unity.

The fact that Rome was the leading city of the world and that the Church of Rome was noted for its charity and generosity, gave the Bishop of Rome a position of precedence and influence. Christians in the West looked to the See of Rome as a court of appeal to ensure fair play when disputes arose, as Christians in the East looked to Constantinople. The primacy and precedence of the See of Rome on historical, not theological grounds, was never disputed by Anglicans, and Anglicans, by and large, have no difficulty in accepting the Pope's primacy of honour which was generally recognised in the days of St Patrick and the Celtic church when Rome was the capital city of a vast worldwide Empire. The city of Rome enhanced the importance and influence of the Bishop of Rome.

We understand how later papal claims to universal jurisdiction originated, for the pattern of the Roman Empire with its strong central authority in Rome in the person of the Emperor, enforcing uniformity by his governors and agents throughout his domains with no place for dissent, became the pattern of the Roman Church with its strong central authority in Rome in the person of the Pope, enforcing uniformity by his bishops and clerical agents throughout the whole church, with no place for dissent or heresy. The infallibility decree of 1870 had a strong political motive in that it was regarded by its proponents as providing a divinely given answer to revolutionary secularism, moral relativism and Christian disunity. When questioned about the witness of scripture and tradition to infallibility without the consent of the whole church represented by the bishops, Pope Pius IX replied, 'What witness? I am tradition.'

A papacy which is a focus of unity expressing the general mind of the whole church, bishops, clergy and people, a universal pastor serving the church from within, as part of the church, not apart from the church, with its pastoral role of service to all, would find a responsive chord in many Anglican and indeed Protestant hearts.

Are we in all our churches inhibiting the exercise of love by perhaps paying too much attention to our theological past and not enough to courageous adventure into the future under the guidance of the Holy Spirit?

Change, process is of the very essence of life. The future is not a mere repetition of the pattern of the past. Not that the past is unimportant. What is of value in it must be conserved to enrich the future – but the future, to be vital and effective, must present a different appearance from the past. A future which merely attempts a repetition of the past is a 'drop-out' in the history of mankind in every sphere of human striving, in art, music, politics, religion, economics, sociology, and so on.

Christianity is not a collection of doctrinal or theological patterns which are repeated in every detail from age to age. If this were so there would be no need for the guidance of the Holy Spirit. Christianity is a way, a movement, a dynamic surging forward of love inspired by the Holy Spirit. Therefore it may well be interesting and at times helpful, but it should never be conclusive, to refer back to what Luther, Calvin or Cranmer said in the sixteenth century, or the Caroline Divines in the seventeenth, or what Pope Pius said in 1870. As it may well be interesting and at times helpful, but it should never be conclusive, to refer back to what Pádraig Pearse or Edward Carson said in 1916.

For all the time the situation is changing, and we can render a great disservice to the advance of charity if we refuse to recognise the reality of change; if we continue to imprint on this present age, ideas and notions which once may have been relevant and valuable, but which are really out of place and out of date in the complex dynamic pattern of social, political and religious life today.

I envisage the united church of the future as including 'Catholic' and 'Protestant' elements in a healthy synthesis. The Catholic element is essential to emphasise continuity of the faith through the visible community of the church through the centuries, and to counteract any tendencies amongst Protestantism to subtract from the substance of the faith 'once for all delivered to the saints' (St Jude). The Protestant element is essential to emphasise the necessity of returning to the witness of Holy Scripture as the bedrock of our faith, to keep the distinction between essential and non-essentials, to emphasise not only freedom of conscience for all but that the church in every age is in need of reformation. Protestantism and Catholicism need each other. They both belong together and neither can banish the other for they both represent authentic elements within the gospel. They have a unity made richer by diversity. Thus, Protestantism is an essential ingredient of true Catholicism. The Christian Church, to be true to its founder, must by its very nature, be universal or catholic, for Jesus is Universal Saviour, Saviour of the world. Therefore, titles such as the Church of Ireland, the Church of England or the Church of Rome, by localisation and limitation, really contradict the catholicity of the gospel. While contributions of Roman, Celtic, Anglican, Orthodox, etc, spirituality in their diversity enrich the unity, Catholicism is greater than any particular manifestation and the Holy Spirit ever leads us onward to deeper insights into the truth of the universal and catholic gospel of Christ.

Authority must be credible and be seen to be credible. Authoritative claims like 'the Bible says so' or 'the church says so and that's final' are not sufficient. We have to ask why does the church say so, or the Bible? Is what they say credible in today's world or do they reflect in certain aspects of their teaching the mind-set of another age? This means that theology must never be isolated from the findings of other disciplines, such as psychology and sociology. In seeking the answers to moral issues in such matters as family planning, contraception, AIDS, sterilisation, divorce, abortion, homosexuality, genetic engineering, embryo research, Christians must have regard, not only to Holy Scripture and Christian tradition, but to the whole body of relevant scientific and empirical knowledge. God expects us to use our intellect, to have vision and foresight and to take the appropriate humane measures to cure or prevent our ills. Answers to complicated moral problems must be arrived at by patient and informed discussion and debate under, as Christians believe, the guidance of the Holy Spirit. There is no shortcut. There is no immediate, simple and final answer supplied by the ready application of such concepts as 'divine' or 'natural' or 'moral' law. The moral law is not something self evident, ready to hand, which can be applied to give a prompt and conclusive answer to every complex moral problem. It is not something imposed on the situation, as it were, from the outside. It emerges from the inside, from the ever-deepening insight into a complex moral issue arrived at by the collective and informed experience of Christians who use their heads as well as their hearts, their intellects as well as any emotional attachment they may have to any particular theological position.

The idea of authority in the Christian Church as a sort of oracle, dispensing infallible and satisfactory answers to every doctrinal or moral problem, is a fiction. We have to work hard, think hard, pray hard to find the answer. Even then we may be mistaken. We cannot be certain. But we can be sure of one thing. If a mistake is made in all good conscience, God in his own time and in his own way will eventually 'correct what is amiss and supply what is lacking', provided we persevere in faith as pilgrims and seekers of the truth. The Holy Spirit ultimately, as promised, guides us to the truth.

Ecumenism and Ordination

Theologians through the centuries have debated the question: 'What constitutes valid ordination?' But most Christians today

are not really interested in this matter. Especially in this ecumenical age it is becoming increasingly evident that, judged by
Our Lord's criterion, 'By their fruits shall ye know them' (Mt
7:16), non-episcopal as well as episcopal ministries have been ef-
fectively used by Our Lord in his service. Ministry is service,
and an ordained ministry which is to serve the needs of whatever kind of Christian unity may in time emerge to replace our unhappy divisions will, I believe, embody the valuable insights
possessed by different Christian traditions, Episcopal, Presbyterian, Congregational and so on. Each has something to contribute to the total enrichment and effectiveness of the work and
witness of the church. Indeed, it may well be that instead of one
form of ministry accepted everywhere and by all, there will be
different forms, some more suitable than others depending on
the circumstances, historic, cultural and racial, of particular
countries or regions.

The ministry is there to serve the church, the people of God,
and true 'apostolic succession', whether episcopal or non-episcopal, is in the people of God witnessing to the teaching and
mission of the apostles. The only criterion of a valid ministry is
how effective it is in promoting Christ's work in the world.

The theory of the divine rights of kings resulted in the popular acceptance of a hereditary monarchy as the only valid form
of government, the very 'esse' or being of the state: no monarch,
no state. Similarly, belief in the 'divine right' of popes or bishops
resulted in the popular acceptance of apostolic succession
through episcopacy as the only valid form of church order and
government, the very 'esse' or being of the church: no bishop, no
church. But no one doubts today the validity of a republican
constitution for any state which so chooses. Equally 'apostolic
succession episcopacy' should be reluctant to question the validity of non-episcopal ministries and thereby to limit catholicity to
Roman Catholics, Orthodox and Anglicans. Catholic consensus
is the consensus of the whole people of God throughout the
whole world who can affirm their common faith by reciting together the Lord's Prayer and the Apostles' and Nicene Creeds.

Vincent of Lerins put it succinctly in 434 AD, 'that which was held always, everywhere and by all, *semper, ubique ab omnique.'*

Most churches claim scriptural support for their particular form of ministry or church government, something for everyone. St Paul, in his first letter to the Corinthians, speaks of apostles, prophets, teachers, leaders, miracle workers, speakers in different tongues, etc. In truth the form of church government eventually arrived at reflected patterns in society.

The absolute monarchy of the papacy, based on divine right, reflected the Roman Emperor as a god at the apex of an imperial pyramid. Here was a ready-made model of a hierarchical system, male, legalistic, uniform and self assured, with the laity at the bottom whose only role was to obey authority without questioning, the authority at the top percolating downwards through its agents. With the rise of democracy the reformed churches became less hierarchical, more democratic and representative of clergy and laity in synodical church government and, in most, women are now admitted to Holy Orders. Anglicanism, while holding on to the traditional orders of bishops, priests and deacons, made episcopacy constitutional, the bishop in council or synod acting, not unilaterally, but in conjunction with elected and representative clergy and laity. Others, like the Salvation Army and Society of Friends, reject the distinction between clergy and laity and have only one form, the ministry of the laity.

The form of ministry in each case was not lifted complete and entire from Holy Scripture. Only later were texts in Holy Scripture solicited and quoted in support of particular types of ministry and church government.

Jesus laid down no definite instructions regarding the church or its government. He was concerned with preaching the kingdom of God, the rule of universal love based on the infinite value of each individual as a child of God. The early Christians expected Jesus to return very soon and accordingly were not greatly concerned about exact forms or valid structures of church government. However, towards the end of the second century, with no immediate prospect of the second coming, the

pattern of the threefold ministry emerged, bishops, priests and
deacons. Some hold that this came about under the guidance of
the Holy Spirit while others claim it simply reflected the hierarchical structure of Roman society and government in descend-
ing degrees of authority filtering down from the top: Emperor –
provincial governors – local administrators – civil servants, paralleled by – Pope – diocesan bishops – parish priests – deacons.
Thus it was natural for this pattern to emerge without any divine sanction or interference. Two views, both sincerely held.
All of which should teach us not to be too ready to unchurch
those whose pattern of ministry does not agree with ours.

If the gender, the 'maleness' of Jesus, is the reason or one of
the reasons put forward for denying the priesthood to women, it
follows that the church, which is as defined by St Paul 'the Body
of Christ' (Ephesians 1:23; Romans 12:5), must on this reasoning
be exclusively male. Since women are baptised into membership
of the church or Body of Christ, gender, whether male or female,
cannot be the deciding factor and it is, to say the least, illogical to
regard the gender of Christ as irrelevant in baptism but relevant
in the issue of ordination. What is relevant is the humanity of
Christ. (Galatians 3:28: 'Neither male nor female but all one in
Christ Jesus.')

Similarly the gender of the twelve apostles cannot be the
defining factor in vocation to the priesthood. There were many
reasons in the customs and circumstances of the first century for
Our Lord's choice of twelve men, who were also Jews, to pioneer
and supervise the missionary work of the primitive church, circumstances which no longer are relevant today. Indeed, if we
were to take Our Lord's choice of the twelve literally and follow
it through in every detail as a scriptural example and obligation,
the church would be reduced to twelve bishops, all male and all
Jewish converts to Christianity!

In the Middle Ages the church had become the exclusive preserve of a male celibate priesthood with a rigid line drawn between clergy and laity. Segregation of clergy from women also
became the norm, especially in the monastic life. Women were

not looked on as partners equally esteemed, but had an inferior role and were seen as a source of sexual temptation. The idea of the church as the whole people of God, an inclusive community, each member of equal worth in God's sight, and all indwelt by the Holy Spirit, was lost sight of.

Ecumenism and Eucharist

The Eucharist is part of the church, not apart from the church, and the church includes all the people of God. The Eucharist is the outward, visible and effectual sign of Our Lord's assurance that where 'two or three are gathered together in my name, there am I in the midst of them'. (Matthew 18:20)

Speculation as to how he is present may be of interest to theologians, for example transubstantiation etc, but is of secondary importance. The crucial fact is that he is present. 'Here our deepest homage paying, We in loving reverence bow, Thou are here, we ask not how', as a well known Anglican hymn puts it. Therefore the whole people of God, in the diversity of their various traditions but with a common faith in the redemptive love of God revealed in the one Jesus Christ, risen and ascended Lord and Saviour, must have equal access to the Eucharist, for it belongs to all. It is as universal as the love of God, transcending all our divisions and denominations. In the Eucharist we are bound closer together in our search, under God, for that richer and visible unity and so Eucharist becomes not an end in itself, but a hallowed means to help us reach that desired goal where 'all may be one, that the world may see and believe'. Catholicism in its very essence must be as wide and all embracing as the love of God revealed in Our Lord Jesus Christ, the Catholic or Universal Saviour, who was not ashamed to sit down, talk and share the table with sinners. The table at the Eucharist is his, not ours, and the invitation comes from him, not us, to his 'sweet feast of love divine'. We read that 'the common people heard Christ gladly' (Mk 12:37), and on the question of intercommunion 'the common people' hear and respond to his invitation and lead the way.

Exclusiveness narrows catholicism by holding Jesus captive in regulations and directives to do its bidding in church or sect. When exclusives, whether of the Protestant or Catholic variety, talk about loyalty to the truth they mean the truth as they see it. Ecumenism, in so far as they recognise it, then becomes ultimately not a joint exploration into 'the inexhaustible riches of Christ", as the apostle Paul says, but the intention to show others the error of their ways and convert them to theirs, the 'one true way' and the only authentic Eucharist.

Eucharistic controversy on a state occasion
In June 1973 the service to mark the inauguration as President of Ireland of Erskine Childers was held in St Patrick's Cathedral. This followed the precedent of a similar inauguration service which Douglas Hyde had requested on his appointment as first President of Ireland in 1938.

My Vicar, Cecil Bradley, and I were invited by Mrs Childers to dinner to discuss the form of service. Erskine Childers made it clear that he wished the service to take place within the context of the Eucharist, the central act of Christian worship. From an ecumenical point of view this presented a problem for some Roman Catholics because in those days the Roman Catholic hierarchy felt uneasy about attending the celebration of the Eucharist or Holy Communion in Protestant churches.

The hierarchy would have preferred an ecumenical service drawn up by representatives from all the churches. But the President elect was adamant, the service must be the Eucharist on this solemn occasion. I totally supported his view and even consulted Archbishop Buchanan of Dublin who agreed that Mr Childers' wish should be paramount. The matter was also raised in the House of Bishops, where the Bishop of Ossory and later Archbishop of Dublin, Dr H. R. McAdoo, won the support of the Church of Ireland episcopate for my decision to have the Eucharist.

As the President is President of all the people in Ireland, I decided to invite leaders of the various denominations to participate in the Eucharist, by assisting in the readings and prayers at the service. Presbyterians, Methodists, Salvation Army, Society of Friends, Moravians, Baptists and others all gladly accepted my invitation. I asked Archbishop Ryan, the Roman Catholic Archbishop of Dublin, if he would give an address or say prayers or read a lesson either before or after the service of Holy Communion or give a special blessing should he feel unable to join the other church leaders in the actual service. I stressed how very much I would like him to participate in the ceremony in whatever way he felt he could, and I assured him that two places in the Sanctuary with the Church of Ireland bishops would be reserved for himself and Cardinal Conway of Armagh.

To my great disappointment Archbishop Ryan was not willing to co-operate. The media, I believe, was to a certain extent responsible for the misunderstanding. When it was announced that I intended inviting representatives of other denominations to participate, the media described it as an ecumenical service. As I was well aware of the strictly technical and restrictive nature of the term as perceived by the hierarchy, I deliberately refrained from using it. So Archbishop Ryan was under the impression that I had advertised an ecumenical service and was trying to slip in the Eucharist under the cloak of ecumenism. The fact of the matter is, I had emphasised that the service would be the Eucharist according to the Order of the Church of Ireland but I was also inviting other denominations to participate.

It should be noted that previous Presidents who were Roman Catholics had their Service in the Pro-Cathedral and this was invariably the Mass. Representatives of other churches were present but were not invited to take part. President Childers and I felt that the Eucharist according to the rites of the Church of Ireland would certainly be in keeping with established precedent, but in our case we wished those from other churches not only to attend but to participate in conducting the service.

The archbishop's reply to my invitation was cool, stating that he and the Cardinal would attend the service but would sit in the nave. They would take no part in the proceedings. I was told by those sitting near them that the archbishop was as good as his word and appeared to take no interest whatever in the Order of Service. But the incident was soon forgotten and the archbishop and I, on subsequent occasions when we met, never mentioned it, nor was it allowed to impair a happy and friendly relationship which I enjoyed not only with Archbishop Ryan, but with his successors, Archbishops MacNamara and Connell. We had our disagreements on theological issues, but differences of conviction should never be allowed to destroy Christian charity. We must speak the truth as we see it, always in love.

An ecumenical service in the technical sense, particularly for the Roman Catholic Church, is one drawn up by representatives of the various churches and agreed by the bishops and other church leaders. Such a service, reflecting the lowest common denominator and without any recognised or recognisable liturgical form, generally fails to impress, edify or inspire. I believe all Christian worship, of whatever denomination, must be ecumenical, for Jesus Christ is Lord of all, Saviour of all. Because of this, Christians who profess to worship him as Lord and Saviour must always welcome, indeed invite, fellow Christians of different traditions to join with them in what really matters, the worship of their common Lord and Saviour Jesus Christ. Jesus Christ is the true ecumenist, the Saviour of the world, the Catholic Christ, having the whole gospel for the whole world.

Ecumenism, thank God, has moved on since 1973. Today Roman Catholic bishops are present in the Sanctuary during the celebration of the Eucharist on such occasions as the ordination of a Church of Ireland bishop. Thirty years ago the attitude of the Roman Catholic hierarchy was that ecumenism should only stretch as far as a jointly agreed service.

It was a source of great sadness to President Childers that he had to go forward alone in that service to receive Communion because his Roman Catholic wife was forbidden by her church to join him. And he was, of course, similarly excluded from receiving the sacrament with Mrs Childers at official functions where Mass was celebrated. On a number of occasions he told me how he could not understand why individuals who wished to partake of Holy Communion should be prohibited by ecclesiastical regulations and decrees from doing so. He felt this could not be in accordance with the mind of Christ.

Of course he was right. We must never lose sight of the fact that it is the Lord's service and the Lord's table, that the invitation to sup with him comes from him alone and not from any priest or any denomination. He is Lord of the sacrament as he is Lord of the church. As I see it, it is the height of presumption for priest or minister to decide who shall be allowed to come and who shall not. All denominations should extend an invitation to every Christian present, and it is a matter for the individual whether he or she accepts or not according to their conscience. Barring people from coming forward because they do not hold a particular theological or philosophical belief as to how exactly Christ is present in the sacrament is, I believe, usurping the place of God and becoming a judge of the worthiness or unworthiness of individuals. Religious legalism is then in command. 'We have a law and by that law he ought to die,' howled a mob stirred up by their religious leaders crying out for Christ to be crucified. They believed it was God's law, divine law, the divine imprimatur. How often is Christ crucified with his love and compassion in the name of the law of the church? We have a law – but God is not in our hands. We are in his.

The ecumenical hope
In January 1977 during his visit to Dublin I invited the world-renowned Roman Catholic theologian, Hans Küng, now alas deprived by the Pope of his official status as a church theologian, to give a lecture in St Patrick's Cathedral to an ecumenical congregation. The cathedral was packed to over-flowing, people stood in the aisles or sat on the floor, and Hans Küng was greeted enthusiastically and loudly applauded by clergy and laity of all denominations.

God never leaves himself without witness. As Hans Küng put it: 'The crisis of the church and its leadership today will be overcome by those who, at this decisive moment in the church's history, despite everything, continue to perform their service in the strength of faith.'

'The dogs may bark but the caravan moves on,' and I believe ecumenism eventually will point to a papacy as a primacy of honour which is a focus of unity, expressing the general mind of the whole church – a papacy inside and a part of the church with the pastoral role of service to all. This pastoral role, as Hans Küng emphasises, will be the mark by which above all else it is recognised and is seen to follow the example of the Good Shepherd, Our Lord himself.

How better to sum up the ecumenical adventure than in the words of Archbishop William Temple (Archbishop of Canterbury, 1942-44):

Always the breath – the wind – of the spirit is moving. We know it by its effect. We have no need to ask for its authentication. Is it Protestant? Is it Catholic? Where the fruit of the spirit is apparent, there the spirit is at work. We should place ourselves in its course that we may be carried by its impulse, even though this leads to association with strange comrades.

While movement at the top may be slow or non-existent, the Spirit is moving at parish level with rectors and parish priests, in an atmosphere of friendliness and mutual respect, leading their people in joint worship, Bible study, and cross-community projects, all witnessing to the unifying power of the gospel. True ecumenism is starting at the bottom, with the common people who, as of old, 'hear Christ gladly'.

One final thought: imagine a truly ecumenical council with representatives of the World Council of Churches and the Roman Catholic Church, presided over by the Pope to discuss matters of common Christian concern. For some, perhaps a majority, the dream ticket of the future. For others, 'a bridge too far'.

Fallacies or mutual misunderstandings

'You Protestants don't believe in the Virgin Mary.' How often have I heard this! Of course it is utterly false. As members of the Church of Ireland we hold the blessed Virgin Mary in high honour as the one chosen by God to be the Mother of Our Lord and as a wonderful example to us of humility and obedience to the will of God. Her hymn of praise, *Magnificat*, is appointed for use daily in Evening Prayer. We observe in our church calendar two special days in connection with the Virgin Mary, 2 February, the Feast of the Purification or Presentation of Christ in the Temple, and 25 March, the Feast of the Annunciation, or the announcement by the angel to Mary that she had been chosen by God to be the mother of Jesus. But the Immaculate Conception, decreed by Pope Pius IX in 1854, that Mary was preserved from original sin, and the Assumption, proclaimed by Pope Pius XII in 1950, that Mary was assumed or taken up into heaven, are not part of the teaching of the Church of Ireland, for these doctrines have no scriptural or historical support. Anglicans and members of the Church of Ireland make a clear distinction between what we see as the essential doctrines of the Catholic faith contained in the creeds, witnessed to in Holy Scripture, held always, everywhere and by all, and later additions such as the doctrines of the Immaculate Conception and Assumption. We regard these later additions as optional extras or pious opinions which may or may not be believed but which are in no way essential to the Christian and full Catholic faith.

It has been said to me, 'You Protestants don't believe in the Body and Blood.' The reference here is to transubstantiation, which is a philosophical way of defining the presence of Christ in the Eucharist or Mass. Certainly we don't believe in transubstantiation but we do believe that Christ is really present in the Eucharist 'in a heavenly and spiritual manner' and that the Body and Blood of Christ are 'verily and indeed taken and received by the faithful in the Lord's supper'. We believe that Christ is truly present but we do not resort to any philosophical formula to explain *how* he is present.

'The Queen is the head of your church.' Another fallacy. The Queen is prayed for in Northern Ireland as the Head of State, as is the President in the Republic of Ireland. The Church of Ireland is autonomous, governed by the General Synod consisting of the bishops, elected clergy and laity. The Church of Ireland is a member of the Anglican Communion which is a family or fellowship of equal, autonomous or self-governing churches in many lands and which claims to uphold and propagate the ancient Catholic, apostolic faith and order without any additions or subtractions. These churches are in full communion with one another and with the See of Canterbury. They look to the Archbishop of Canterbury, not as Pope or supreme ruler, but as one among equals who nevertheless occupies a position of considerable esteem and honour. Neither the Archbishop of Canterbury nor the Queen has any authority over the Church of Ireland.

'Your church was founded by Henry VIII.' Wrong again. Henry VIII was never a theological reformer. Indeed, he wrote a book against Martin Luther for which the Pope gave him the title 'Defender of the Faith'. He lived and died an opponent of Protestant Reformation theology, however much he may have quarrelled with the Pope over the annulment of his marriage. Politics and the national interests of England, Spain and the papacy played a leading role in the attitude of both Henry and the Pope. Henry made himself 'Head of the Church' in England, not to make it Protestant in theology, but to reject papal interference in the political affairs of England. There would have been a Reformation had Henry never lived, for Reformation was in the air in Germany, France, Bohemia, Switzerland, etc. Henry supplied the spark which kindled the fire of the Reformation in England but, had he not done so, others certainly would have, for Reformation was inevitable. The aim of the Anglican reformers was not to found a new 'Protestant Church' but to purge the church of innovations which they felt had no foundation or justification in Holy Scripture or ancient Catholic practice.

And it is not all on one side. Protestants are also guilty of misunderstanding and malice, evident from such remarks as, 'Roman Catholics worship idols and images', or 'Roman Catholics worship the Virgin Mary and make her greater than God for they call her the "Mother of God"', 'Roman Catholics can sin as much as they wish provided they confess to the priest who forgives them and leaves them free to sin over and over again with a clear conscience … and they reject or at least devalue the Holy Scriptures.' 'If the Pope is infallible and so powerful, why doesn't he stop war and violence? 'The Church of Rome is the great whore of Babylon, drunk with the blood of the saints …'

The Book of the Revelation, chapter 18, is the happy hunting ground for those who loathe the Pope and Church of Rome – 'living in luxury, ruling as a Queen – all the nations have drunk of the wine of her fornication'. But for those fanatical hate-filled Protestants, there is eventually cause for rejoicing for there will descend on the Pope and his apostate church plagues, pestilence, mourning and famine and finally destruction by fire 'for mighty is the Lord who judges her'. (Rev 18:8)

These old canards, both of the Roman Catholic and Protestant variety, so prevalent in my schooldays and producing suspicion and hatred, can still be heard from time to time, in spite of the ecumenical movement and its laudable attempts to remove misunderstanding and to create an atmosphere of mutual respect which can only come by the removal of ignorance of what each really believes and why.

Anti-agreement and anti-ecumenical Protestants

The Protestant community in Northern Ireland is bitterly divided. I would estimate that at least fifty per cent regard all Roman Catholics with suspicion, if not outright hostility. The Protestant ascendancy mind set, nourished by the Orange Order, cannot come to terms with what they see as concessions to the nationalist Roman Catholic community. Roman Catholics in their eyes are the allies of republicanism, bent on destroying Protestant Ulster, a perception reinforced by widespread anti-ecumenism

amongst many Protestant clergy and laity and Dr Paisley's dia-
tribes against popery and the Roman Catholic Church, which he
insists is not a Christian Church at all. In spite of this, or perhaps
because of this, Paisley and his Democratic Unionist Party can,
at elections in a polarised society, muster such a substantial
Protestant vote as to constitute a real threat to the less extreme
Ulster Unionist Party. Anti-Catholicism is also fed by the fact
that such 'renegades' as Roger Casement, having embraced republicanism, proceeded to convert to Rome. Further proof, they
say, of the alliance between republicanism and Rome. It's also
worthy of note that Casement grew up in North Antrim, now
Ian Paisley's constituency!

All this sets the stage, in times of tension, for hotheads consumed by hatred and perhaps fortified by alcohol or drugs, to go
out, maim or murder Roman Catholics indiscriminately. Such
vile deeds are of course promptly and rightly condemned by
Protestant leaders, civic and religious, and are utterly abhorrent
to the Protestant community as a whole. But the Protestant population also see the rapidly increasing vote for Sinn Féin
amongst Roman Catholics and the murders of Protestants by
their military wing, the IRA, which took place particularly in
border areas, as evidence of an anti-Protestant sectarianism and
genocide of the Protestant community. While republicans and
their supporters, conscious of the fact that many leading republicans such as Tone, Emmet, McCracken and Mitchel were
Protestants, claim that their 'armed struggle' was directed not
against Protestants, but against their British and unionist identity,
such claims have a hollow ring for Protestants who, regarding
unionism as part of their heritage, see these attacks as an assault
on their Protestantism. And in Northern Ireland it's the perception which counts.

Religion and the 'Real Irish'
Many nationalists and republicans in Northern Ireland are descendants of the Scottish or Cromwellian planters. A change in
religion, from Presbyterianism to Roman Catholicism, brought

them into 'the other tribe'. After the Reformation, Rome became the ally of Irish Catholicism against 'heretical' English Protestantism and the planters or their descendants who converted, usually through marriage, to Rome also changed their political allegiance. Conversely some native Irish Roman Catholics, mostly to their political advantage, converted to Protestantism, usually to the Church of Ireland, and became part of the unionist tribe. Religion in Ireland became the defining and divisive factor in deciding political allegiance and national identity.

The British and Protestant settlers of the past had in their ranks the ancestors of many fervent republican families today, as also the subjugated native Irish Catholics had in their ranks the ancestors of many fervent unionist families today. Only when religion enters the equation does the question of who are 'the real Irish' arise. Irishness as synonymous with Roman Catholicism rules out Protestants. (Britishness as synonymous with Protestantism rules out Roman Catholics.) Exclusiveness enters with religion. Scant regard is paid to history or ancestry. Tribal boundaries are rigidly defined, politically and theologically, and apartheid or separation frequently degenerates into suspicion and hatred. 'Enough religion to make us hate.'

There are of course some who have 'bucked the trend', Protestant nationalists and Catholic unionists, but these are in a minority in Northern Ireland. Nevertheless they witness to the wholesome attitude that Irishness should transcend religious or party political allegiance, that neither Roman Catholicism nor Protestantism should be used to justify an exclusive political claim to Irishness on the one hand or Britishness on the other.

The alleged ancestral garment, whether of the orange or green texture, does not fit easily on the shoulders of many in Northern Ireland today. In truth, we are a mongrel, mixed up and myth-fed people, and the idea of a 'one true authentic Irish tribe' is a romantic fallacy.

St Patrick: Roman Catholic or Protestant?

I once witnessed a St Patrick's Day parade in New York in which
St Patrick was featured on a huge banner complete with mitre,
pastoral staff and episcopal garments festooned with sham-
rocks. Immediately following was another banner demanding
'Brits out of Ireland' and I wondered about the fate of St Patrick
himself, surely a most distinguished Brit. Would he be the first
candidate for retrospective expulsion and ethnic cleansing?
Here St Patrick was being hijacked and portrayed as anti-British,
anti-Protestant, and the very embodiment of Roman Catholic
triumphalism.

At the opposite end there is the extreme Protestant evangelical
picture of St Patrick, seeing him in his *Confession* as immersed in
Holy Scripture, totally surrendered to Christ, no mention whatever of the Blessed Virgin Mary or of papal authority and, for
good measure, coming from Britain, the son of a deacon and
grandson of a priest.

What can we say about our patron saint? Who was the real St
Patrick?

We know for certain that St Patrick could not have dressed as
a modern bishop since such garments were not invented for at
least 500 years after Patrick's time. Much of what is attributed to
St Patrick is the result of legends which evolved in succeeding
centuries. There is no historical evidence for his alleged use of
the shamrock in explaining the Trinity, or his climbing Croagh
Patrick, or his sojourn on Mount Slemish, or his encounter with
King Leary at Tara. Neither is there solid incontrovertible evidence that he founded a church in Armagh and that he is buried
in Downpatrick. All this is from later sources. For there is a gap
of 200 years between the time St Patrick lived and wrote his
Confession and when people began to write about him, and so
the oral tradition had abundant time to be corrupted by legends,
some of which were used in the cause of ecclesiastical policy to
bestow importance on a place or monastic institution.

It is generally agreed that Patrick was born in Britain at a
time when it was one of the outposts of the Roman Empire. As a

member of an aristocratic family of Roman citizenship, he had the advantage of a Roman education with knowledge of the Latin language and Roman literature. When nearly sixteen he was captured by Irish pirates who brought him to Ireland where he spent six years tending sheep.

He then escaped from Ireland and later returned as a bishop and spent the remainder of his life evangelising in Ireland where he died. That's all we know for certain. The rest is legend, theory, speculation, conjecture.

While nowhere does St Patrick mention the papacy or that he was sent as a bishop to Ireland by the bishop of Rome, it is highly unlikely that he would have wished to set up a church in Ireland totally independent of the Roman Church, especially at a time when Rome was the centre of a widespread Empire and knowledge of Latin, Roman law and literature essential for 'the upper classes'. Therefore the claim that he would have favoured a totally independent Celtic Church can hardly be sustained. He was content to go along with the prevailing ecclesiastical order provided it did not interfere with his evangelising mission to preach Christ as Lord and Saviour. Christianity in Ireland, as it later developed in its Celtic form, liked to do things in its own way as shown in its monastic structure and divergence from continental Roman Christians in, for example, the date of Easter and mode of tonsure. His utter devotion to the centrality of Christ and the complete absence of any reference in his writings to the Virgin Mary, invocation of saints, etc, would seem to indicate that such a man as Patrick, whose faith was centred solely on Christ and who was inebriated by the Holy Scriptures, would hardly have been an enthusiastic champion of later papal decrees and doctrines which had no warrant in Holy Scripture. So there is something to be said on both sides and neither has an exclusive claim on St Patrick. Instead of being divisive, St Patrick can be a focus of unity, accepted and honoured by all.

'The strong name of the Trinity' speaks to us of unity in diversity, parity of esteem and creative interaction generating love instead of confrontation, and all reflected in the Godhead, highlighting for us the only way to peace and reconciliation.

Education

The question of integrated education, understood in Ireland as the education of children of different religions together, should concern all who seek to heal the wounds of a divided community.

In a community where religious differences between Christians do not run deep (as in Britain or France) denominational schooling will have little or no effect on the status quo. Whether a pupil attends a Roman Catholic School or a Church of England school is of no more relevance, as far as the community is concerned, than the game he chooses to play or the club he chooses to join. Where no division already exists on political, national, cultural or racist grounds, denominational schools will certainly not create one. But the story is different where the community is deeply divided on political and religious lines as in Northern Ireland. Here division is perpetuated by educating children separately in denominational schools. The Christian Churches profess to be committed to reconciliation and the removal of strife and division in society. One would expect them to have taken the lead in promoting the cause of integrated education which, when all is said and done, is the practical expression of the Christian gospel of one family under the one Fatherhood of God. Unfortunately all the churches have acquiesced in, and sometimes encouraged, the tribalism of their adherents, with resultant tension and divisiveness in the community. At the very outset we implant unwittingly in young innocent minds a 'them or us' attitude which can rapidly become 'Thank God we are not as the others. We are the elect, the chosen ones.' 'We are right, they are wrong.'

Education has a crucial role in ridding our land of intolerance. Only a fool would claim that integrated education is the complete answer. But to meet together, to talk together, to learn together, to play together, to be together must surely help to remove ignorance, prejudice and misunderstanding. The teacher of history to a mixed class of Roman Catholics and Protestants will be more alive to the danger of a one-sided presentation and the need to be absolutely fair to all sides than a history teacher in a denominational school. Integrated education helps children to recognise the fact that people do have different points of view and that we must be as tolerant of their point of view as we expect them to be of ours.

Do we hear too much from the churches on the need to preserve a 'Protestant ethos' or a 'Roman Catholic ethos' and too little about having a common Christian ethos expressed in being together and practising together the Christian virtues of tolerance and mutual understanding without which reconciliation is impossible? Far from this being a watering down of the gospel, it is highlighting its great central theme, love of God and love of my neighbour, with all its practical implications for the individual and society.

In Northern Ireland if the education of children together from the earliest years and from different religious backgrounds had received the support and goodwill of the churches and government, as envisaged by the first Minister for Education, Lord Londonderry, one is bound to ask – would so much ignorance, suspicion and vitriolic hatred of the 'other side' have been largely avoided, with little or no support for the paramilitaries, whether republican or loyalist, whose impressionable minds, tunnel vision and segregated sectarian ardour have brought so much suffering, especially to the innocent? Words of the Most Reverend James Doyle, Roman Catholic Bishop of Kildare and Leighlin in 1826 are relevant today: 'I do not see how any man … can think that peace can ever be permanently established … if the children are separated at the commencement of life, on account of their religious opinion. I do not know of any measure that would prepare the way for a better feeling in Ireland, than uniting children at an early age and bringing them up in the same school, leading them to commune with one another and to form those little intimacies and friendships which often subsist through life.'

Failure to live up to our Celtic heritage

For Celtic Christianity the power and presence of God shone throughout the whole creation.

The veil between heaven and earth, the supernatural and the

natural, had a sensitive and delicate transparency. That other world was forever intruding on this one. Eternity was continually bursting into time. The outward and visible, the whole panorama of nature, like the bread and wine in the Eucharist, pointed to an inward and spiritual grace. The spiritual and the material were but the two inseparable sides of the same coin of reality. Nature, the whole creation, was sacramental. In all our churches today we have overlooked or minimised this fact, the great truth that since all things come from God, we are stewards and trustees of God's creation. We have detached nature from grace, the world from God.

The theology of creation has been largely overlooked in favour of the theology of redemption. Personal salvation for Protestants and doctrinal ecclesiastical obedience for Roman Catholics have been the hallmarks of religion in Ireland, especially in Northern Ireland. Exploitation of the environment for greed, pollution of all sorts, the disfiguring of towns, countryside and seaside by litter and rubbish, have become accepted as normal, as a way of life, prompting no concern or sense of civic responsibility, even awareness, on the part of so many who would also claim to be Christian. Responsibility strictly limited to home, garden, car, but outside this private domain let others deal with the problem and clean up the mess.

This disposable and dependency mentality was given added impetus by the 'Troubles' in Northern Ireland which led to a withdrawal from the public arena devastated by bombs, into the isolation, privacy and comparative security of house and home, resulting in responsibility for the outside or public environment being regarded as the affair of others. And the churches to their discredit have gone along with this without raising an eyebrow. Yet it goes to the very heart of the gospel. For when people cease to respect and care for God's creation they are well on the road to losing respect for all God's creatures, including those created in God's image, and with loss of respect 'man's inhumanity to man' rears its ugly head and soon opens the floodgates to strife and bloodshed.

In a word, we have in the churches stood the Bible on its head. Instead of beginning with Genesis and the old creation, we have turned to the Revelation or Apocalypse, concentrating on the new spiritual creation and isolating it from the old. The Celtic Christians were more scriptural and held fast to the continuity between Genesis and Revelation, the earthly and the spiritual, creation and redemption, thereby displaying a wonderful reverence for nature and the environment, 'the work of an almighty hand' and all permeated by his divine power and presence.

Ecumenism and Final Solutions

Where we can, let us in the churches reach out together into the community in joint action in tackling environmental and social questions, such as the prevalent dependency culture and drug problem. And surely we in the churches, through our leaders and representatives, should at least discuss and try to achieve some degree of consensus or common mind on such crucial moral problems as abortion, divorce, homosexuality, euthanasia, contraception, genetic research and reproduction, etc. Now, if consensus on all or some proves impossible, then the churches, in a spirit of honesty and tolerance, should publicly recognise that on complex moral issues, different views are sincerely held by committed and well-informed Christians of all traditions. None of us must judge or condemn those who see things differently. All must call for tolerance, mutual respect and charity and each must avoid the 'holier than thou' attitude which can only damage our common Christian endeavour.

History has shown how unwise and, in the long term, detrimental to Christianity has been absolutist moral positions taken by the church without due regard to all relevant factual or scientific evidence, not only its treatment of Galileo but also in its frowning initially on the practice of using anaesthetics, blood transfusions and transplants. Even the church has its u-turns.

Any system, church practice or policy asserted or imposed by reference to authority, even divine authority, and shielded by the authorities from rational examination in the light of contemporary knowledge and experience, is really a non-starter in today's world.

Christians must always be open to the possibility of change, remembering that the church in all its branches has in the past opposed changes which it later sanctioned. So we must listen not only to the past, to traditional doctrines and practices, but to the experience of people today both inside and outside the Christian community. Listen to the past, but not fear the future. Fear is the great motivator in authoritarian systems, fear to risk the security and certainty of the present for the possible insecurity and uncertainty of the future. But God is a risk taker and he expects us also to take risks, to try things out, to get things wrong, to make mistakes, for only in this way can we mature to freedom and fulfilment. And all the time we are surrounded and sustained by God's love, 'in whose service is perfect freedom'.

Jonathan Swift ridiculed those who believed in final, absolutist systems, utopias to solve all problems with neat and tidy answers. No system, theological, political, etc, is perfect. All 'isms' have their little day and then give way to something else. We can only strive for the least imperfect in an imperfect world, and the least imperfect is that which increases respect for human dignity and freedom and decreases the amount of suffering. In this way, by promoting tolerance and compassion, we love God and our neighbour.

CHAPTER 4

What sort of God?

After Constantine, God became like Caesar, imperialist, all powerful, demanding complete obedience, annihilating dissent. And Jesus was looked on as the conquering hero, the protector of imperial armies battling under the Cross to ensure the triumph and universal acceptance of the 'one true religious and political faith'.

This concept of a God of power and exclusion and protector of 'his own', 'his chosen ones', has infected all the institutional churches. For example, in Northern Ireland there is, for many, an imperialist God, Protestant or Catholic, giving exclusive sanction to either unionism or nationalism, orangeism or hibernianism, and there is 'the deification' of doctrinal texts or confessional statements where keeping 'the true faith' really becomes synonymous with assent to dogma, whether of the Catholic or Reformed variety.

But God is always beyond our concepts and definitions. As infinite, God can never be fully comprehended by us. If we could fully comprehend God, then God would not be God and we would not be finite human beings.

How we speak of God must always be partial, never final, the last word. For churches to claim finality or absolute certainty for their partial understanding leads to exclusiveness and religious self-righteousness which can easily, when mixed with tribal politics, degenerate into sectarianism. With such baggage only a spark is needed to produce the hideous spectacle of sectarian violence with 'enough religion to make them hate', and a God, their God, all powerful, trampling their enemies under foot. A God, their God, used simply as a means, a weapon, with no thought or intention of Christian worship or obedience. Instead an arrogant ignorance of the gospel.

What we can all be sure of is the message of Jesus, the exhortation to love God and love my neighbour, all ultimately stemming from a God of love. A God of love is a vulnerable suffering God, a God who in humility stoops to take on himself the nature of humanity and who in Jesus weeps at the injustices and cruelties of man's inhumanity to man. This is the God whom the churches must proclaim and embrace. As with Christ, churches should be humble, suffering, vulnerable, risk taking, prophetic rather than dogmatic and absolutist, preserving the institution at all costs.

Penal Laws, Persecution and Forgiveness
'I am profoundly glad that the grievances of Roman Catholics are removed and I recognise and deplore the injustice of their lot before that time. The penal laws were the product of quite other times. In some countries one side imposed penal laws; in some countries the other did. It happened that in England and in Ireland penal laws were imposed by a Protestant government; but the laws they imposed were all of a piece with similar laws enacted against Protestants elsewhere. It was the existence of such laws against Protestants in France that brought great bodies of French Protestant refugees to find a new home in Ireland. I make no pretence to justify penal laws. I would ask that those who have the teaching of the youth in Ireland should not teach history in a false perspective by concentrating attention on what happened in Ireland to the exclusion of what was happening simultaneously elsewhere in Europe. It is only natural to feel most keenly about hardships inflicted on and suffered by those from whom we are sprung. A reading of the history of France and the Netherlands, of Spain, of England, and even of Ireland, would show that positions were in some cases reversed, and that then it fell to the Protestants to suffer. I do not think any one has anything to gain by dwelling on the hardness of those past ages.'

Archbishop Gregg: Address to Dublin Synod, 1929.

The argument from persecution is not the exclusive preserve of any one denomination. Every denomination has its martyrs. Religious persecution is a stain on the history of Christianity, an evil out of which no denomination should seek to make capital but for which all should be penitent before God and ask forgiveness one of another. Sorrow, penitence, forgiveness not only for the persecution and oppression of others, but for failure for whatever reason, usually self interest, to condemn persecutors and tyrants and reluctance to take a stand alongside the persecuted in the name of Christ and common humanity.

Generosity, trust and forgiveness
Trust and transformation can only be achieved by reaching out to others in a spirit of generosity – exactly as God did when he reached out to us 'while we were still sinners', as St Paul puts it. Words of Archbishop Desmond Tutu come to mind: 'Never be afraid to talk, because when people sit down and talk to each other they discover each other. Old obstacles seen in the light of a new relationship become less formidable and progress is made.'

The apartheid 'them and us', 'lost and saved' syndrome with its Judaeo conditional morality, I'll only talk if you do (a) or (b) or (c) etc, is still very much out and about in Northern Ireland. We must take risks in reaching out across the divide. While dialogue may not solve the problem, it is at least a necessary first step, an essential ingredient in the solution.

As Christians following the generosity of Christ, we in the churches should have encouraged the rotation of municipal offices such as Mayor or Chairperson between the political parties in corporations and councils. In the old days, unionists would not even have a nationalist as Deputy Mayor in Derry. Generosity of spirit as commended in the gospel would have gone a long way to ease bitterness and tension in our divided society. It's sad to think that this rotation only began when nationalists and other non-unionists took control of councils. Unionists in solid control never shared power and yet these unionists for the most part were active churchgoers, loyal members of their re-

spective churches, who saw no contradiction between this and
the gospel imperatives. Politics and Christianity were placed in
different compartments. Enough religion but little Christianity
and condoned by the Protestant churches without any protest or
embarrassment.

We in the churches must acknowledge and accept our share
of blame for the 'troubles'. 'Did that play of mine send out certain men the English shot?' asks Yeats. Did words of hatred in
school or church or home, Protestant or Roman Catholic, send
out men and women to murder? If so, when we sit in judgement,
remember we too share in their guilt. All churches must in humility ask God's forgiveness, and forgiveness from one another
and from the victims and families who have suffered so ap-
pallingly, not least because of the religious and political sectarianism which we in the churches, to maintain our power and status,
have so often inculcated or encouraged or condoned. Our com-
munal guilt demands repentance and that our judgement be
seasoned with mercy in deciding on such sensitive matters as
the release of convicted terrorists. Ancestral voices of sectarian
religion and politics, the voices of exclusiveness, self-righteousness and hatred of others have played no small part in putting
them behind bars and, while they are there, we cannot have an
easy conscience. None of us has clean hands.

James Stephens (Irish storyteller and poet) wrote: 'There is
no tragedy more woeful than the victory of hate for hate is finality and finality is the greatest evil that can happen in a world
where movement is the very essence of life. For hate slams the
door on life, killing the hater. It is a contradiction of the essential
dynamic of life and so is always negative, stagnant, suffocating,
self destructive.'

Hatred corrupts the hater. But forgiveness does not come
easily, especially when you have seen innocent members of your
family or friends cruelly murdered in cold blood by terrorists.
Forgiveness is not a sentimental thing. You don't have to like the
people you forgive. On the contrary you may find them repugnant, not to be trusted and so on. You may dislike intensely, but

you must also love intensely, more a matter of the will than of the feelings. So when we forgive, although we are far from liking that person or what he has done, at the same time we recognise in him or her a child of God, one whom God loves, one for whom Christ prayed and died, and we likewise pray and hope and strive in every possible way that by the grace of God that person may, as the prodigal son did, come to himself, arise and return to his Father by accepting the forgiveness of God so freely offered on the Cross. We may not like, we must love, and if we love we must desire for him that which God desires him to be. And all the time aware of our own shortcomings and failures for we are all sinners and fall short of the glory of God. (Romans 3:23)

In Judaism there was the belief that you could only offer forgiveness where there was first of all a genuine repentance on the part of the sinner, emphasis on repentance as a condition of forgiveness. But Jesus put the emphasis on forgiveness 'while we were still sinners' (Romans 5:8), God reached out to us in Jesus. The gift of forgiveness (giving forth love) is freely offered and we are at liberty to accept in repentance or reject it. God in Jesus always takes the initiative. Grace is freely offered as in baptism and we have to make the response, 'choose ye, whether to accept, forsaking the old, embracing the new or reject it out of hand'.

William Blake, the mystic, asked what makes Jesus unique when compared with great teachers, Plato, Aristotle, Cicero, and he answered: 'Forgiveness of sins, this alone is the gospel, the light and immortality, brought to life by Jesus.'

Forgiveness, as we have said, does not come easily, especially when we are confronted with the intense suffering or death inflicted by criminals on loved ones and other innocent victims. The salutary and very proper desire that the perpetrators shall be speedily brought to justice and subjected to the full rigors of the law may be accompanied by the desire for revenge. The victim consumed by hatred finds it impossible to forgive. Nor is the acceptance of forgiveness always easy, the recipient too proud to accept and be humbled by a sense of shame and guilt. Indeed, he may feel no tremor of conscience whatever, being convinced that his actions, however obscene in the eyes of the community, were justified by 'the cause' to which he was committed.

For forgiveness to be effective, there must be a turning away from the proud ego of self-righteousness to that lone figure on the Cross who emptied himself of all pride and self-seeking and showed us on Calvary the extent to which the forgiving love of God is prepared to go, even without any response on our part, 'while we were still sinners', and calls us by God's help to do likewise, for God never gives up on the sinner. This is the challenge of the gospel, unique and formidable. This in Blake's words '*is* the gospel' quite unlike anything gone before.

Amid all the strife, suffering and sorrow, we find hope and encouragement in the example of people like Gordon Wilson who so movingly forgave those who had cruelly murdered his daughter in the Enniskillen Remembrance Day bombing. Faith, hope and love shine through in innocent people so willing to forgive and pray fervently that others, of whatever creed, colour or class, may be spared a mother's or father's grief. Here is the gospel in action. Enough religion to make us love.

CHAPTER 5

The Big Issue: Abortion

The abortion referendum and religion

The Pope arrived in Ireland on 29th September 1979, and we arranged an ecumenical vigil in St Patrick's Cathedral, Dublin on that night for peace and reconciliation. It was well attended. We hoped that the Pope would put in an appearance but a crowded and overrun schedule prevented this. However, Cardinal Willebrands, Head of the Vatican Secretariat for Christian Unity, came along, as did Bishop Birch of Ossory and other members of the Irish Roman Catholic hierarchy.

During his visit the Pope condemned the use of violence in Ireland to achieve political ends and also spelt out clearly his opposition to artificial birth control, divorce and abortion. With his conservative Polish background, the Pope was concerned about the growing support for change to a more open and pluralist society in the Republic and the increasing readiness to question papal directives on certain moral and theological issues, such as contraception, divorce and the ordination of women. On abortion the Pope had the support of PLAC, the Pro-Life Amendment Campaign, founded in April 1981, which brought together conservative or right-wing Roman Catholics to press for an amendment to the Constitution which would guarantee the right to life of the unborn.

Public opinion was firmly against legislation of abortion, and no politician had ever suggested such a thing. Yet to rule out the possibility, however remote, of abortion being legalised in certain cases, PLAC demanded a Constitutional amendment completely prohibiting abortion. The instability of government during that period – with three general elections in the space of eighteen months – greatly assisted the efforts of PLAC to ensure sympathy and support for their proposal from the main political parties, Fianna Fáil and Fine Gael. Labour, while also sympathetic, held that this was not a party matter and should be dealt with by means of a free vote. Dr Michael Woods, Minister for Health in the Haughey administration which was in office from March to December 1982, produced the proposed wording of the Constitutional amendment two days before the collapse of the twenty-third Dáil. Although Dr Garret FitzGerald would have preferred the amendment to be considered with other possible amendments to the Constitution and not taken in isolation, nevertheless the powerful lobby of PLAC extracted a pledge that the new Fine Gael-Labour coalition government under the leadership of Garret FitzGerald would introduce legislation to adopt, by 31 March 1983, the pro-life amendment published by the outgoing government. This had the backing of the two largest parties in the Dáil. The parliamentary Labour Party reserved the right to a free vote on the issue.

The wording of the proposed amendment was:
The State acknowledges the right to life of the unborn and, with due regard to the equal right to life of the mother, guarantees in its laws to respect and, as far as practicable, by its laws to defend and vindicate that right.

While the then Minister for Justice, Michael Noonan, said that the government would consider changes in the wording provided they retained the underlying principle that the practice of abortion should not be permitted to creep into Irish law, Michael Woods for Fianna Fáil defended his party's wording and stated that 'when the amendment was published we were entitled to believe that we had secured the general support and agreement of the Church of Ireland and of the Catholic Church at the highest levels ...' Whatever about the agreement of the Church of Ireland 'at the highest levels', I certainly could not agree to the proposed wording, and in a statement to the newspapers in February 1983, I set out my misgivings. This led to an interview with Brian Farrell on the television programme *Today Tonight*, innumerable messages by phone and post, mostly congratulatory but some very critical and vindictive, calling me a pro-abortionist, a child of the devil, an angel of death, a Herod advocating the massacre of innocents. I appeared on public platforms as a member of the anti-amendment campaign, including the great concluding rally in Liberty Hall. There were only two Church of Ireland clergy in the anti-amendment campaign, the Reverend Peter Tarleton from Limerick and myself.

Peter was a long-standing friend and admirer of the late Limerick stalwart, Jim Kemmy TD, and the three of us occasionally met and lunched together in Dublin during the Dáil sittings, for we had many common interests and aspirations. Although some prominent members of the Church of Ireland, such as Catherine McGuinness, Shane Ross, Mary Henry, Trevor West and David Norris, were active in the anti-amendment campaign, many Church of Ireland people were, to say the least, puzzled by statements from Fianna Fáil giving details of three separate meetings involving the Archbishop of Dublin, the Most Reverend Dr McAdoo, with government representatives while Fianna Fáil was still in office. It was claimed by Fianna Fáil that Archbishop McAdoo had accepted the wording but asked for time to consult the Archbishop of Armagh, Most Reverend Dr Armstrong, who was said in turn to have also accepted the wording and expressed gratitude for the efforts made to meet Protestant wishes. Garret FitzGerald, in his autobiography (p 417), states that 'it has since been confirmed that the draft was shown to and approved by the Church of Ireland Archbishop of Dublin'. Successive governments, if all this is true, did not understand the workings of the Church of Ireland. Whereas in the Roman Catholic Church, archbishops or the episcopal conference can call the tune and speak on behalf of their church, in the Church of Ireland the final authority is the General Synod, consisting of the bishops, elected clergy and laity, with its Standing Committee responsible for day-to-day decisions when the Synod is not in session. Knowing the archbishop very well over the years and having a high regard for his integrity, I can only conclude that he was acting with the full authority and approval of the Standing Committee, and in a laudable effort to avoid unseemly controversy and divisiveness, had approved the wording.

The first public intimation by the church that any talks on the amendment had taken place was given in a statement by the Standing Committee in November 1982, which said: 'We recognise that an attempt has been made to take account of the complexity of the subject and the views expressed by our own and other churches'.

Another statement in July 1983 expressed 'appreciation at having been included in the general consultations held by successive governments'. The Archbishop of Armagh further stated in an RTÉ interview that 'the Church of Ireland had accepted the original wording in the beginning and was very pleased to have been approached by both governments for their opinions'. Meanwhile, there was mounting opposition to the wording, not only by certain committed and loyal members of the Church of Ireland, but by Protestants of other denominations and, more significantly, by a great number of liberal Roman Catholics who were looking to the Church of Ireland and Protestantism in general to give a lead in the anti-amendment campaign.

The Standing Committee, having apparently approved the wording, could only set out certain things to which no-one in the Church of Ireland would object, such as repeating the statement made at the Lambeth Conference of 1958 and 'in the strongest terms Christians reject the practice of induced abortion, or infanticide which involves the killing of a life already conceived (as well as a violation of the personality of the mother) save at the dictate of strict and undeniable medical necessity'. They added the comments that a Constitutional amendment would not alter the human situation in the country or contribute to its amelioration, and that Constitutional prohibitions were not a way to deal with complex moral and social problems. But there was no detailed examination of the proposed text, critical or otherwise. Only this morsel of advice: 'given that a referendum is to be held, a responsibility devolves on all citizens to play a full and constructive part in expressing their views on its wording'. Time and time again during the campaign, I was accused of being out of step with my own church. Since my own church in its Standing Committee was giving no clear public lead on the proposed wording, I found it hard to believe that I was out of step. How can one be out of step with a motionless object? On the other hand, from the letters, telegrams and phone calls which I was continually receiving, it was obvious that if anyone or any group was out of step with the views of the Church of Ireland, it was the Standing Committee. The anti-amendment campaign condemned the proposed wording as sectarian. Indeed, in order to be approved by the Roman Catholic hierarchy, which it was, the wording had to reflect Roman Catholic teaching, so denominationalism was inevitable and inescapable.

It was said by my critics that nowhere did the Standing Committee refer to the wording as sectarian, 'therefore it was not sectarian, according to the Church of Ireland'. This was easily countered by pointing out that nowhere did the Standing Committee pass judgement on the wording. Silence ruled. It had nothing to say as to whether the wording was sectarian or non-sectarian.

Because of what they had come to believe were dangerous ambiguities in the wording of the amendment, the FitzGerald government now produced an alternative:

Nothing in this Consitution shall be invoked to invalidate
or to deprive of force or effect a provision of the law on
the grounds that it prohibits abortion.

The Standing Committee did say that this was preferable to the original amendment on the grounds that the original wording 'it has been suggested might have to be interpreted by the courts'. At a time when the possible interpretation of the words was of crucial importance to the Church of Ireland, it grieved me that no clear and explicit lead was forthcoming from the Standing Committee on the ambiguity and implications of the wording. At times during the campaign I felt deserted, shunned, an embarrassment to the Church of Ireland.

The Roman Catholic hierarchy opposed the alternative wording, and threw it weight behind the original which was endorsed by the Episcopal Conference in August 1983. Unlike the Church of Ireland, the Roman Catholic leadership did not hesitate to spell out clearly its position and give a lead to its people, as it was perfectly entitled to do. The Church of Ireland was on record throughout the 1970s as advocating a more open, tolerant and pluralist society. Therefore to be true to itself and to the cause it publicly espoused, it should have taken more seriously and more courageously what so many who supported the anti-amendment campaign perceived, and rightly so, to be a threat to the whole idea of pluralism. One Church of Ireland bishop wrote to me giving full support for what I was saying: my good friend Noel Willoughby, Bishop of Cashel and Ossory. A few clergy also wrote in support and one or two in condemnation. They thought I was advocating wholesale abortion on demand! But most backing came from Roman Catholics, priests and people, who wanted our society to move in a more pluralist direction and to have done with any elements of confessionalism in our Constitution. The Church of Ireland laity who took the trouble to inform themselves and examine the situation gave me eager support and encouragement, but sadly it must be admitted that large numbers of Church of Ireland people were totally indifferent, and many were confused by the insidious propaganda labelling all who were against the amendment as pro-abortion, and by the absence of a clear lead from the Standing Committee. The Role of the Church Committee, which dealt with political and social issues, and of which I was a member, congratulated me after one of my TV interviews and expressed unanimous approval of what I had said. This was reported to the media by the then Southern Secretary of the Role of the Church Committee, Mr Trevor Matthews, and appeared on RTÉ news. Within the hour both of us had phone calls from a church official demanding a withdrawal of the TV report on the grounds that only the Standing Committee had the right to issue reports to the media. This, as we say, was news to me, and since the TV report was simply a statement of what actually happened at a meeting of the Role of the Church Committee, and there was no infringement of any pledge of secrecy, we refused point blank to accede to the demand. The subject was never mentioned again.

In a debate in the Dáil, Mr Oliver Flanagan TD, referred to me as another Paisley: 'It is enough have one Paisley in the north without having another down here.' Strange logic, I mused, when Mr Paisley's supporters so often referred to me, while in Derry, as a Fenian, a Lundy, a traitor to the Protestant cause!

At the referendum the amendment received the support of 66.45 per cent of those who voted. But only 53.67 per cent of the electorate went to the polls, which meant that of the total electorate in the state, only one-third signified their approval of the amendment, and this in spite of the issue being presented as a choice between good and evil, God and Satan. However, the fact that the pro-amendment vote was double the anti-amendment one indicated that there was no intention, at least on the part of the majority, to move in a pluralist direction or to accommodate a minority view. But considering the size of the anti-amendment vote and the very large number of abstentions, in spite of misrepresentation of the anti-amendment case as tantamount to advocating child murder, the result, I wrote, 'is not without some grounds for hope that one day the Republic will move towards a more open and tolerant society affording mutual respect and recognition to all, majority and minority alike'.

Three years later there followed the divorce referendum. While the Church of Ireland has always been committed to the sanctity of marriage, it recognises the fact that in some cases marriages do break down irretrievably and that the state has a duty to recognise and deal with such situations. There are circumstances in which divorce may be the lesser of two evils. The marriage may be dead. The Church of Ireland therefore supported the removal from the Constitution of the prohibition on divorce. In May 1986 the Dáil and Seanad passed the requisite legislation for a referendum to seek an amendment which would remove the Constitutional ban on divorce. Polling day was set for

Thursday, 26 June. The Roman Catholic hierarchy came out strongly against divorce. Supporters of the amendment were often accused of advocating divorce 'at the drop of a hat' and there was the scare about property rights, all of which resulted in the rejection of the amendment by a 63 per cent majority. While the Roman Catholic Church gave a clear lead in pastoral letters and episcopal utterances, as it was once more perfectly entitled to do, the Church of Ireland failed to spell out clearly to its members that this, like the abortion referendum, was a crucial issue for the cause of pluralism in society, a cause which the Church of Ireland Synods and Committees had repeatedly espoused. No pastoral letter was forthcoming from our bishops. Some Church of Ireland members fell victim to the dirty campaign which labelled those who wished to remove the Constitutional prohibition as being in favour of easy and widespread divorce. Indeed, I received letters from two members of the Mothers' Union accusing me of 'advocating a divorce-ridden society completely contrary to the teaching of Christ and the gospel'.

During the controversies of the early seventies, I had the complete support of the then Archbishop of Dublin, Alan Buchanan, formerly Bishop of Clogher, who knew and understood the north and repeatedly encouraged me by phone calls and letters. The Church of Ireland clergy, apart from those who were members of the Cathedral Chapter and others who had served in Northern Ireland like the Rev Billy Gibbons, Rector of Kill 'o the Grange, a former curate of mine, were seemingly indifferent to, or unaware of, the important question of the kind of society we wished to have in the Republic. No mention was made in occasional conversation with me about anything I had said. One felt there was a deliberate attempt to avoid the subject. Some clergy doubtless thought I would make the Church of Ireland unpopular with the Roman Catholics. So the majority of the clergy confined their interests to their parishes, kept their heads down, said neither yea or nay. They simply did not wish to know.

The parochialism of the Church of Ireland was painfully obvious at the time of the Dublin Crisis Conference. I was shocked to discover that most Church of Ireland members in parishes, especially on the outskirts, were totally unaware of the decay of the inner city and had not the remotest idea of the issues involved in the controversy over the proposed dual carriageway outside St Patrick's Cathedral. The narrow 'I'm all right, Jack' attitude reigned supreme. Their vision extended no further than the parish boundary. The Dublin Corporation did not then include even one member of the Church of Ireland, a telling indictment of the lack of civic spirit amongst the majority of church members. Thankfully, there were a few praiseworthy exceptions. At every available opportunity I urged Church of Ireland youth to take a greater interest in politics and public life, instead of opting out like little Jack Horners.

At that time it seemed to me that the Church of Ireland was scared stiff of controversy. There was an attitude of complacency or resignation. There was one issue, however, which touched the hearts of all Protestants in the Republic – the future of the Adelaide Hospital. The proposal that the 'Protestant' Adelaide should leave Peter Street and become part of a large new hospital planned for Tallaght set the alarm bells ringing. What was to become of the Protestant ethos which respected the privacy and primacy of the doctor-patient relationship, without interference from a hospital ethics committee reflecting the ethical teaching of the Roman Catholic Church? The Protestant position was set out clearly time and time again in Synod, assemblies, committees, by bishops and individuals, lay and clerical.

It was emphasised that on such intimate matters as sterilisation or contraceptive devices and family planning, the person concerned should have the right to make the decision as to treatment after consultation with medical personnel and, if advisable, with the spouse or immediate family. The churches, of course, must have the right and opportunity to provide spiritual counselling if sought. Chaplains should be available, but the decision must ultimately and conscientiously be taken by the patient.

There was also the question of training Protestant nurses.
The Adelaide evoked considerable regard and affection among
many who were not members of the Church of Ireland, particularly in the Liberties of Dublin. Its doors were open to all, of
whatever creed or none. Its emphasis on the direct patient-con-
sultant relationship, with no ethical committee having a veto
standing in the wings, had the support and approval of many
Roman Catholics who did not see eye to eye with the official
teaching of their church on some sensitive, sex-related matters.

It is sometimes argued that Roman Catholic teaching on sex-
related matters is not really sectarian, in that it serves the interests of what is termed 'the common good' of society. At times
the concept of 'the common good' is appealed to as a kind of
axiom, the truth of which only the morally blind can fail to see,
and the notion of the common good in Irish society has strong
sexual overtones. But the morality or 'common good' of society
cannot be narrowed to the sphere of sexual morality. There is no
precise mathematical formula by which to measure the degree
of morality in society. No-one can logically say that a society
which prohibits divorce or sterilisation or abortion under all circumstances has a higher moral tone than one in which such
things are permitted with adequate safeguards under certain
circumstances. If we are to attempt to make a judgement on the
morality of a society or on 'common good', other factors must be
taken into account, such as the measure of individual freedom
and tolerance, the extent of compassion and caring and the commitment to social justice and honest dealing in the community. I
believe the primary aims of any society must be to minimise suffering and to maximise tolerance or, in a word, to exercise compassion and to respect human dignity. The prophet Micah can't
be bettered when he summed it all up: 'To do justly, to love
mercy and to walk humbly with thy God.'

Concentration on questions of sexual morality in Ireland encouraged in society an attitude in which all morality was reduced
to sexual matters, and other vital moral issues such as honesty,
business integrity or social justice were regarded as of only sec-

ondary importance. The unfortunate result was the general feeling among the populace that there was little to be afraid of or feel guilty about, especially in public life, provided any act of sexual impropriety, as defined by the church, was avoided or undetected. We are living with the consequences of this today in the investigations of so many Tribunals in the Republic.

The 1983 Abortion Referendum
Pluralism and True Republicanism

At the concluding rally in Liberty Hall on 2 September 1983, when I was joined on the platform by Michael D. Higgins and Monica Barnes, I said:

This unfortunate and unnecessary referendum has put a great strain on our tolerance and on our tempers. It has divided the whole community – lawyers, doctors, churches. Bitter words have been spoken, smear and scare tactics, emotive misrepresentation are the order of the day and Christian charity is the first casualty. St Paul exhorts us always to speak the truth in love, and to recognise the right of everyone to their views and to show tolerance to one another.

I speak as a Protestant and member of the Church of Ireland. I spent most of my ministry, nearly twenty-three years, in Northern Ireland. There I witnessed the sad results of religious segregation and sectarianism. Certain religious leaders in Northern Ireland believed that they had a 'hot line' to the Deity. They believed that they had a divine sanction to impose their will on the whole community, for according to them it was God's will and God's commandment. Even in sport and recreation where they appealed to the commandment 'to keep holy the Sabbath day' they insisted that, for example, the children's swings should be chained in the parks on Sundays and the swimming pools closed. This they held was God's law, they knew it, and no one had a right to offend against it. And so, having the Northern Ireland experience behind me, I am very much alive to the danger of doing anything which might seem to advance in any way the cause of sectarianism in the Republic. I do not want Protestant sectarianism in Ireland and I do not want Roman Catholic sectarianism in Ireland. I want Christianity in Ireland. Swift said: 'We Irish have enough religion to make us hate one another but not enough (Christianity) to make us love one another'. We need less religion in Ireland and more Christianity.

I am pro-life and like the vast majority of Protestants in Ireland, both north and south, I am utterly opposed to abortion on demand – indiscriminate abortion – as a means of birth control or simply to terminate an unwanted pregnancy. But no Protestant Church or Protestant organisation has campaigned for the inclusion of this amendment in the Constitution. Why? Because Protestants feel that the law governing abortion is really a matter for the Dáil. Abortion is already illegal under present legislation, the 1861 Act. In this the existing law reflects public opinion. If the law proves defective in doing this, it can quickly be changed by an Act of Parliament.

The Constitution is another matter. Protestants feel that the Constitution should keep clear of controversial moral issues. It should have wide acceptance, being the expression of a common unity and consensus, and it should avoid divisive issues. Such issues should be a matter of legislation, after debate and decision by the Dáil, and not a matter for the Constitution. No Protestant Church or Protestant organisation campaigned for this referendum. On the contrary, all the Protestant Churches have made it abundantly clear, time and time again, that they are opposed to the holding of this referendum. The Roman Catholic Church on the other hand is strongly in favour and the Dáil has concurred with the Roman Catholic hierarchy's point of view. Therefore, whether we like it or not, at the very outset sectarianism was introduced into the question.

When the referendum was inevitable Protestants unanimously supported the Fine Gael proposed wording, as being more acceptable from our point of view. This would, we feel, have met the stated intention of the pro-life group in that it would have prevented any possibility of the Constitution being invoked to legalise abortion.

The Protestant Churches had compromised, when faced with the reality of the referendum which they from the outset had opposed, but even this compromise was insensitively rejected by the Dáil and the Roman Catholic Church and we were left with the original Fianna Fáil wording. The rejection of the Protestant Churches' willingness to compromise in an effort to solve this sorry problem can hardly be seen as an act calculated to reduce the sectarianism implicit in this whole business.

To turn to the present wording. Protestants see the present wording as ambiguous. Medical and legal experts disagree as to the possible consequences, if this form of words is inserted into the Constitution. We feel that on such an important question there should be no ambiguity, no uncertainty. The electorate should know exactly what it is being asked to vote for. And Protestants feel that there is a dangerous ambiguity. No Protestant would maintain that a mother has only an equal right to life to her unborn baby. For us the mother's right to life is superior and primary. Where there is a conflict, the rights of the mother's life and health must take precedence over that of the unborn child. Her rights must be the primary concern, for she is in a real sense the heart and core of the family.

Also if the term 'unborn' is to be identified, not only with the foetus, but with a fertilised ovum, then there is a grave danger that certain forms of contraception acceptable to Protestants will be declared unconstitutional on the grounds that they are 'abortifacients'. The question is therefore how the courts will interpret the amendment if passed.

The pro-life people say that there will be no change in existing medical practice and that contraception will not be affected. They may be right. But they may be wrong. Legal and medical experts differ. Therefore, to say the least, there are very substantial grounds for uncertainty. We simply do not know what the courts will do.

As I understand it, the pro-life people want this amendment to guarantee the right to life of the unborn, but they would allow two exceptions, where the life of the mother is endangered either by (1) an ectopic pregnancy or (2) cancer of the uterus. These are the very exceptions, and the only exceptions, recognised by the Roman Catholic Church and justified on the debatable theory of what is known as the principle of double effect, since the intention is the removal of the life-threatening cancer or abnormality. But from the point of view of the foetus (or the unborn), whether the killing is direct or indirect is irrelevant. The crucial fact is that the unborn is killed. Therefore, even in the absolutist Roman Catholic teaching, the killing of the unborn is justifiable under certain conditions. 'A rose by any other name ...'

If these are the only exceptions to be permitted in an amendment prohibiting abortion, then it is difficult to see such an amendment as non-sectarian, for such an amendment would enshrine in the Constitution only the Roman Catholic position. Such an amendment could hardly be regarded as non-sectarian when it would rule out other exceptions, which might be judged on medical grounds to threaten the life of the mother and which are acceptable to non-Roman Catholics. Thus, the generally held Protestant ethical view which would allow abortion as a last resort in certain unfortunate exceptional cases, on the grounds of strict and undeniable medical necessity, would be narrowed and restricted by the Constitution. Protestantism is suspicious of rigid legalism and absolutism in dealing with complex moral issues. The individual case is all important and must be seen in the wider context of the sanctity of all human life and the mother must always be treated with compassion and Christian concern.

On this question of sectarianism, I am not saying that it was the intention of any political party or the Dáil to make this a sectarian issue. What I am saying is that by the very nature of the problem it was impossible to avoid a sectarian dimension to this debate. First of all there was a sectarian division on the very nature of the Constitution and secondly, while there is a general agreement amongst Roman Catholics and Protestants that indiscriminate abortion is morally wrong, Protestants would not be so rigid as the Roman Catholic Church as to the exceptions to be permitted. Protestants would judge the matter of exceptions on the ground of strict and undeniable medical necessity where the mother's life or health is at risk. Thus, it was impossible to produce a form of words to accommodate the rigid Roman Catholic point of view. The best that could be done was to Constitutionalise the present position, thus avoiding the need to produce a positive, definite form of words.

This was tried by Fine Gael, accepted by the Protestants but rejected by the Roman Catholic Church and the Dáil. Sectarianism was unavoidable. I have said from the beginning, over and over again, that it was impossible to produce on this issue a non-sectarian wording.

We have to ask ourselves the question: What sort of state do we want? Do we want a confessional state on Roman Catholic lines or a pluralist society in the true republican tradition of Tone and Davis? We can't have it both ways. In truth, the proposed amendment has little to do with the question of abortion which is already prohibited by law. It has everything to do with the question of whether we are to enshrine in the Constitution a particular ethical view on certain moral issues. This I maintain is not properly a matter for the Constitution.

I do not want a Protestant confessional state in Ireland. I do not want a Roman Catholic confessional state in Ireland. Sectarianism and confessionalism have been the curse of Ireland, north and south, for far too long. I want a truly tolerant and pluralist Ireland. I will not desecrate the graves of Tone and Emmet, of Davis and Edward Fitzgerald, of Isaac Butt and Parnell, and of all the other Protestant patriots who helped to form and fashion this nation. These were men of wide and tolerant vision. There are those today who would turn that vision into a sectarian squint. I will not tarnish the memory of Shaw and Yeats, of O'Casey and Douglas Hyde and of all the other Protestants who have made a marked contribution to the cultural, artistic and intellectual life of this nation. And because I will not do this, I will vote *No* in this divisive, sectarian, unnecessary and futile referendum. And I hope all you who have the good of the Irish nation at heart will do likewise.

Over the grave of Swift in St Patrick's Cathedral there are these words: Go traveller and imitate if you can one who played a man's part in the cause of liberty.'

I appeal to you in the cause of liberty to vote *No*.

Theological differences
The Roman Catholic view that a human being or person comes into existence at the moment of conception in the fertilised ovum is not generally accepted by Protestants. The Protestant would say that a fertilised ovum is a human life with the potential of becoming a human being or person, as the acorn, though not an oak, has the potential to become one. So there is a gradual development from fertilised ovum and embryo to foetus, right up to the moment of birth. No consensus exists as to what point exactly there is a human being, a person, a child present. To define 'the unborn' as a human person at the moment of conception is to enshrine a particular theological position in the Constitution. If this is upheld by the courts then it follows that all abortifacients, such as the 'morning after pill', become illegal and those found using such devices are guilty of performing an abortion. But I cannot see the common sense of the common people ever equating the abortion of a fertilised ovum with the deliberate killing of a baby and, as such, exacting the same sentence of life imprisonment for murder. It is now becoming crystal clear that no amount of referenda will ever produce a satisfactory solution to this very complex, intensely personal and emotional problem. While there is certainly no demand in Irish society for 'indiscriminate abortion', there is at the same time a growing unease about an absolutist or total prohibition, with the realisation that such a personal and intimate problem demands a non-judgemental approach to those who are the victims of such total prohibition, and a feeling that a compassionate society has no right to inflict such suffering upon them.

Epilogue

In St Patrick's Cathedral Dublin there is an old medieval Chapter House door. It's called the door of reconciliation. In the middle of the door is a large hole. In 1492 two Irish noblemen, the Earl of Kildare and the Earl of Ormonde, were engaged in violent conflict and Ormonde and his followers took refuge in the Chapter House. Kildare was anxious to end the quarrel and he asked Ormonde to open the door and shake hands. Ormonde however was suspicious – 'you can't trust them – they're all the same' – whereupon Kildare took an axe, cut a hole in the door and reached out his arm through the hole and embraced the hand of his enemy, Ormonde. It is said that the phrase 'chancing your arm' comes from this incident. Kildare chanced his arm. He realised that conflict between two families living in the same country, worshipping the same God but filled with hatred, each trying to wipe the other out, was utterly opposed to what each professed as Christians. 'They had enough religion to make them hate, but not enough to make them love.'

Tribalism and sectarianism always lock the door, find security in the past, define themselves by exclusion and refuse to associate in worship or to engage in politics with others who do not share their religious or political opinions.

Those who show real Christian courage and conviction are the Kildares of this world. They take the initiative, make the first move, often at risk not only from the enemy without but from the more confrontational members of their own side within. Here is the gospel of Christ in practice, for God in his love reached out to us in Christ and says to each one of us 'Go and do thou likewise.'

Therefore as Christians, true to our calling, we must resolve to seek reconciliation rather than recrimination, co-operation rather than confrontation, inclusiveness rather than exclusiveness. To us is committed the ministry of reconciliation. But tribalism rejects reconciliation in favour of confrontation and victory over the other side, or at least keeping them 'in their place'. In spite of the opening up of Irish society, north and south, to Europe and the world, the old tribalism still shows itself in both jurisdictions when it comes to the crunch, for example in dealing with civil strife and policing. The gut reaction is 'we mustn't let our side down'. The sad fact is that, although there are some exceptions especially amongst the professional classes, the nationalist or republican tribe is broadly identified with Roman Catholicism and the unionists with Protestantism. Politicians encourage this tribalism when they see themselves as representing Protestants or Catholics instead of all their constituents. Religion is the tribal badge, 'enough religion to make us hate', a mindset nourished by the failure of institutional religion, on both sides, to give courageous Christian leadership and reinforced by the partition of the country into Protestant unionist and Catholic nationalist.

While praiseworthy efforts are made by ecumenical Christians in both tribes to cross tribal boundaries – bringing children together for holidays, co-operation in various social and charitable endeavours – nevertheless while we in a divided society continue to place children in separate schools on denominational grounds in their earliest and formative years, the tribal mentality is perpetuated and tribalism, however concealed in normal day to day contacts, emerges in all its true colours at parliamentary and local government elections. However much individual Protestants or Roman Catholics may dislike the official candidate or candidates on election day, the pull of the tribe ensures that the vast majority of the electorate vote either Protestant/ unionist or Catholic/nationalist or republican, in spite of the valiant efforts of smaller parties like the Alliance to cut across tribal boundaries.

What of the future? The British/unionist/Protestant tribe, increasingly middle aged and elderly, is in decline, unable even to replace losses due to death and emigration of their youth, a decline which will become ever more rapid in future years, with more and more Roman Catholics moving into areas once solidly Protestant. If this trend continues, in twenty years or so Protestants will no longer be in a majority and the future will lie in the hands of Roman Catholic/nationalist/republican elected politicians whatever they may decide for the province. A united Ireland can't be taken for granted. But one thing is certain, whatever form the future relationship of the province with the neighbouring island may take, Northern Ireland will be primarily and officially Irish, with Britishness as an optional extra for those who wish to claim it. Considering a united Ireland, the question arises: Would the twenty-six counties have a welcome 'on the mat' for the six? Many will ponder on Hilaire Belloc's warning:

And always keep a hold of nurse

For fear of finding something worse.

With the growth of secularism, the rejection of authoritarianism in religion or politics and the falling off in numbers and influence in the institutional churches on both sides, the political incentive to attendance (keeping our end up) will no longer operate and tribalism and sectarianism will gradually fade.

Time, with Irishness losing its Roman Catholic identity, less institutional religion, changes in demography and the emergence of a European and global mentality especially among the youth, together with increased facilities for travel, mobility and interchange of ideas, will all play their part in the final withering away of the cruel sectarian divisiveness which prompted Swift to pen those terrible words: 'In Ireland – enough religion to make us hate. Not enough to make us love.'

Sources

Frederick Augustus Hervey, 4th Earl of Bristol. Bishop of Derry (1768-1803).

Jonathan Swift, *Thoughts on religion and various subjects* (1728).

William Blake, *Songs of Innocence* (1789).

J. E. Acton, *Essays in the Liberal interpretation of history* (1890).

Tertullian (160-225), *Apologeticum*.

Augustine, Bishop of Hippo (396-430), *Against the Donatists*.

Pope Boniface VIII (1294-1303), *Unam Sanctum*:

> 'There is but one Holy Catholic and Apostolic Church outside of which there is no salvation or remission of sins and we declare, announce and define that it is altogether necessary for salvation for every creature to be subject to the Roman Pontiff.'

Pope Innocent III (1198-1216), Climax of the Medieval Papacy and claims to ultimate authority in both spiritual and temporal affairs.

Erasmus (1469-1536), *In Praise of Folly* (1509).

Luther (1483-1546), *Peace of Augsburg*. Subjects should follow the religion of their rulers. State established churches.

Calvin (1509–64), *Institutes of the Christian Religion* (1536).

W. E. H. Lecky, *Democracy and Liberty* (1878).

Richard Hooker, *Laws of Ecclesiastical Polity* (1594).

Benjamin Whichcote, Cambridge Platonist. (1609-83)

Roger Williams (1603-83): Banished from Massachusetts, founded Providence, Rhode Island, USA.

Lord Baltimore (1580-1632): founded Maryland, USA.

William Penn: founded Pennsylvania and Quaker colony in Philadelphia (1682).

Pope Gregory XVI (1831-46).

Pope Pius IX (1846-78), *Quanta cura* encyclical, *Syllabus of Errors* (1864) and Papal Infallibility (1870).

Pope Leo XIII (1878-1903), *Apostolicae Curae* (1896).

Pope John XXIII, Second Vatican Council.

J. A. Costello and inter-party government (1948), Message of homage to the Pope, more deferential than that sent by de Valera in 1932. It said:

On the occasion of our assumption of office and of the first Cabinet meeting, my colleagues and myself desire to repose at the feet of your Holiness the assurance of our filial loyalty and of our devotion to your August Person, as well as our firm resolve to be guided in all our work by the teaching of Christ, and to strive for the attainment of a social order in Ireland based on Christian principles.

The Minister of External Affairs, Mr MacBride, represented the government at the opening of the Holy Year of 1950 in Rome, and Ireland was also officially represented at the proclamation of the dogma of the assumption of the Blessed Virgin Mary in November 1950.

Noël Browne, *Against the Tide* (1986).

J. H. Whyte, *Church and State in Modern Ireland (1923-70)*.

J. H. Bernard and J. E. L. Oulton, *The Roman see in the fourth and fifth centuries* (1942).

Irish Bishops in the House of Lords opposed to the disestablishment of the Church of Ireland: Marcus Beresford (Armagh), Richard Chenevix Trench (Dublin), William Alexander (Derry), Robert Knox (Down), James O'Brien (Ossory).

J. T. O'Brien, *The case of the Established Church in Ireland* (1867).

Journals of the General Convention of the Church of Ireland (1870-71).

Journals of the General Synod of the Church of Ireland (1871-1922).

Resolute opposition to Home Rule Bills as 'a threat to the Protestant Faith'. On third home rule bill (1912), a special meeting of the General Synod resolved 'unswerving attachment to the legislative union now subsisting between Great Britain and Ireland'. Only five members, out of over six hundred opposed.

Covenant against home rule in Ulster, 28 September 1912. Supported by five out of six bishops in Ulster.

J. H. Bernard, *The present position of the Irish Church* (1904).

G. Seaver, *John Allen Fitzgerald Gregg, Archbishop, a biography* (1963).

James Stephens, Broadcast Talks (1937-45).

Papal Infallibilty: Popes Liberius (357), Zosimus (417), Honorius (638), Pius V (1615), Urban VIII (1623) all found guilty of heresy or misleading the church: Liberius of Arianism which minimised the divinity of Our Lord, Zosimus of Pelagianism which minimised the necessity of divine grace in human activities, Honorius of monthelitism which said Jesus had one will, part human and part divine, Pius V and Urban VIII: Both condemned Gailileo's views as heretical.

Vincent of Lerins (434): The Catholic faith is that held always, everywhere and by all. The faith is based on consensus and formulated by a General Council, not by any individual Pope or bishop.

R. B. McDowell, *The Church of Ireland 1869-1969* (1975).

Peter de Rosa, *Vicars of Christ: The dark side of the papacy* (1988).

John Cooney, *John Charles McQuaid, Ruler of Catholic Ireland* (1999).

A. T. Q. Stewart, *The Narrow Ground* (1989).

F. S. L. Lyons, *Culture and Anarchy in Ireland 1890-1939* (1979).

Maurice Hayes, *Minority Verdict* (1995).